THE GREAT LOUISVILLE TORNADO OF 1890

I0822205

THE GREAT LOUISVILLE TORNADO OF 1890

KEVEN MCQUEEN

Published by The History Press
Charleston, SC 29403
www.historypress.net

First published 2010

Manufactured in the United States

ISBN 978.1.59629.892.7

Library of Congress Cataloging-in-Publication Data
McQueen, Keven.
The great Louisville tornado of 1890 / Keven McQueen.
p. cm.
Includes bibliographical references.
ISBN 978-1-59629-892-7
1. Louisville (Ky.)--History--19th century. 2. Tornadoes--Kentucky--Louisville--History--19th century. I. Title.
F459.L857M38 2010
976.9'44041--dc22
2010002063

Notice: The information in this book is true and complete to the best of our knowledge. It is offered without guarantee on the part of the author or The History Press. The author and The History Press disclaim all liability in connection with the use of this book.

Dedicated to Ronda Foust and her son Eli Stansberry.
May they never reap the whirlwind!

Contents

They Contributed, Whether They Know It or Not

Laura All, Geneta Chumley, Drema Colangelo, Eastern Kentucky University Department of English and Theatre, Eastern Kentucky University Interlibrary Loan Department, Lee Feathers, Julie Foster, Rosie Garcia-Grimm, Tom Grazulis, Ken Grimm, Joe Hardesty, the *Louisville Courier-Journal*, the Louisville Free Public Library, the Darrell McQueen family, Kyle and Bonnie McQueen, Pat New, Amy Purcell, Gaile Sheppard, Mark Taflinger, Mia Temple, the University of Louisville Archives and everyone at The History Press. Also: the Conductor.

This book was edited by Lee Feathers of the Green Pine editorial services. www.greenpineeditorial.com.

PART I

Before

As is well demonstrated by Thomas Grazulis's website "The Tornado Project," Americans have always had to fear death dropping from above in the form of nature's most terrifying and violent storm. The earliest recorded American tornado struck Massachusetts on July 5, 1643—and it's all been downhill from there.

Part of the charm of reading old newspapers is seeing how our ancestors tried to explain and prevent these storms. A Mr. Barham, writing in the scientific journal *Nature* in 1877, opined that tornados formed when winds from the north and south "pass[ed] each other on the left hand respectively." In the same year, Professor John H. Tice explained in a truculent article in the *St. Louis Republican* that, contrary to what other scientists and laypersons thought, a tornado's destructive force came not from the wind it generated. Tice felt that tornados bent metal by somehow converting it to a "semi-fluid state." In April 1890, General A.W. Greely, the head of the United States Signal Corps—the nineteenth-century equivalent of the National Weather Service—theorized that large, well-built cities would serve as barriers to a cyclone's winds: "[T]he writer believes a number of closely built brick or stone blocks, where each structure is so substantially built as to withstand tornadic winds without support from the adjacent buildings, may be considered tornado-proof." Farmers could ward off tornados by planting trees as "windbreaks," thought Greely. (Sad experience has taught us, of course, that tornados can and will strike large, well-built cities if they feel like it and consider large trees hors d'oeuvres rather than barriers.) The idea that tornados could be thwarted if large walls were built west of major cities appealed to many; in 1896, Sergeant Dunn of New York's Signal Corps office pointed out the absurdity of this idea, which would require a wall "about as high and broad as a mountain range, and its cost would make the national debt look insignificant by comparison."

But perhaps tornados could be blown up with dynamite? Such was the plan of Professor H.A. Hazen of the Weather Bureau. In 1896, Hazen proposed that a line of lookout stations be placed in areas that were apt to be hit by the storms. Hazen believed that touching off dynamite at the stations by means of wires would blow approaching funnel clouds "to smithereens"—or, at the very least, the explosions would deprive tornados of the electricity he thought necessary to fuel them. "Fifty years hence, not a big town in the southwest will be without a tornado trap," Hazen confidently predicted. In 1899, Chicago artist E.D. Betts released a diagram of his invention, the "cyclone annihilator," which he claimed would dissipate a tornado. The device was a cannon with an attached weather vane and air trigger. When a wind of over sixty-five miles an hour hit the vane,

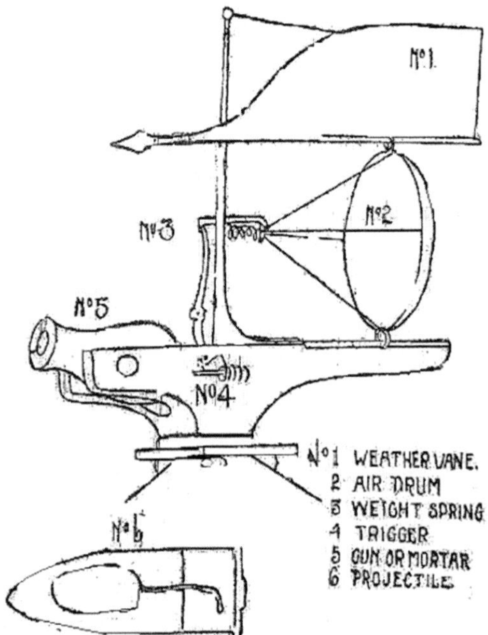

Diagram for E.D. Betts's "cyclone annihilator." Try it if you want to. *Louisville Courier-Journal*, June 25, 1899. *Courtesy of the* Courier-Journal.

it would pull the trigger and fire a projectile into the approaching tornado, which was expected to "throw it off its balance and scatter it into a harmless zephyr." The imaginative artist-inventor added, "I should not hesitate to face the most destructive twister with a common pistol." It is possible that somebody tried Betts's scheme and found it useless—if the experimenter survived, that is.

Scientists still do not fully understand the atmospheric conditions that cause tornados to form, but it is known that the most powerful of the storms develop from supercell thunderstorms. Supercells contain a rotating column of air called a mesocyclone far above the earth's atmosphere. The trouble begins, it is believed, when heavy descending air forces the rotating mesocyclone down to the earth's surface. The rotating air column sucks up dirt and debris, darkens and becomes recognizable as a tornado. Some are long, thin and rope-like; some are hidden behind a wall cloud; some assume the classic funnel shape; and some take on the intimidating wedge shape. Luckily, most violent thunderstorms do not produce tornados; most of the twisters that are formed are weak and dissipate after doing minimal, if any, damage. The average tornado is 250 feet wide and produces winds of between 40 and slightly over 100 miles per hour. Most travel a few miles, lose their strength and disappear. The more formidable tornados, however, can be 1 mile wide, stay on the ground for hours, travel many miles and produce winds of over 200 miles per hour. The highest recorded wind speed from a tornado was 310 miles per hour, measured during the storm that devastated Moore, Oklahoma, on May 3, 1999.

All fifty of the United States have had tornadic activity, though residents of certain regions (especially the Midwest) have a lot more to worry about. Despite not being located in the nation's infamous "Tornado Playground," Kentucky has received its fair share of these violent storms. Richard Collins noted in his 1874 *History of Kentucky*:

> *The tornado is the highest manifestation of the irresistible force of the raging elements, and even in Kentucky, we experience enough to know that only the most substantial of structures or the everlasting hills can defy its power. It is, however, a source of consolation to know that its visitations in Kentucky are not very frequent,* [and] *that, when it does appear, the track over which it passes is narrow, and that it seldom, if ever, travels twice over the same path.*

Collins correctly asserted that tornados are powerful, tend to travel a narrow path and are relatively infrequent in Kentucky. Tornados, however, can travel the same path repeatedly and with impunity, as illustrated by the events in Pittsburg, Kentucky, described later.

Kentucky has a long history of tornadic activity from colonial days up to the present, including the notorious "super outbreak" of April 3, 1974, which resulted in tornados—many of them deadly—striking Richmond, Brandenburg, Louisville and a number of other Kentucky towns, not to mention dozens of communities in twelve other states. However, I have chosen to describe the state's most notable pre-1890 tornados so that the reader will have the same familiarity with their history as residents of Louisville had in the year of their great disaster.

Cave City in Barren County is noted for its proximity to Mammoth Cave, one of the natural wonders of the world. Just before dawn on January 17, 1870, the town was visited by a different, deeply unpleasant sort of natural wonder: a tornado that killed five people. Some corpses were carried three hundred yards. Three more were mortally wounded and thirty others injured. Over fifty families were left homeless. The tornado destroyed every house on the five-mile stretch between Cave City and Glasgow Junction, killing nine in addition to the five dead in Cave City. On January 24, the Kentucky legislature donated $5,000 to the victims.

Between 3:30 and 4:00 p.m. on March 25, 1884, the neighboring towns of London and Pittsburg in Laurel County encountered a storm described as "the severest ever known in this section of the country." The residents of London got off relatively easily. There, the new Methodist church was leveled, and other buildings were less severely damaged. Pittsburg received the storm's full impact. It first hit and instantly destroyed the Aetna Coal Company's tip-house, causing an estimated loss of $1,500. As if to show that it did not play favorites, the twister then struck John Pitman's residence and barn and inflicted $3,000 worth of damage to the Pitman Coal Company. It wrecked the Laurel Coal Company's storehouse (also at a cost of $3,000) and swept away the Peacock Coal Company's tip-house (cost, $5,000). The storm destroyed several cottages where the Peacock Company's miners lived, leaving behind a tangle of broken furniture and clothing. T.C. Stringer's store was marked for destruction; flying debris fractured both of Colonel C.W. Stringer's legs and broke his wife's hip.

The most spectacular damage occurred at the train yard. Three freight boxcars, two tanks full of coal oil and a caboose were blown off the railroad track and thrown down an embankment. A brakeman for the Louisville and Nashville Railroad happened to be standing on a boxcar when the tornado struck. Some accounts give his name as John Hailman, others as Hartman. However, the newspapers' failure to spell his name correctly was the least of the brakeman's worries. He was swooped off the boxcar and blown headfirst into a creek fifty feet away. The impact broke his neck, and he died instantly. Three other lives were lost in the storm: Mrs. Broughton, the wife of a Peacock Company employee, and her two children were killed when the winds demolished their cabin. Five others, including the Stringers, were thought to be mortally wounded.

After the storm dissipated, a heavy, cold rain fell, adding some generalized short-term misery; more serious problems were brought about by unemployment when one hundred coal miners found themselves out of work until the storm damage was repaired in mid-April. In the weeks after the disaster, panicky Pittsburgians fled for the safety of the mines every time a storm formed.

Pittsburg had barely recovered from this major tornado when it was hit by another one on the night of March 27, 1890—the same date as the Great Louisville Tornado. The 1890 twister closely followed the path that its predecessor had traveled six years before. It was a spectacular nighttime tornado, described as being "of inky blackness, and…illuminated by incessant flashes of lightning." It was powerful, causing considerable property damage (including giving Mr. Madison Wells's roof the biggest adventure of its life by carrying it half a mile). It was much larger than the 1884 storm, creating a path of destruction about half a mile wide. This time, however, no lives were lost. On November 14, 2007, Pittsburg encountered yet another tornado that touched down about a mile west of town. The two-hundred-yard-wide tornado walloped the community with winds estimated at between 86 and 110 miles per hour. It traveled about two miles on the ground and damaged a couple dozen structures. No one was killed or severely injured. As the 1884, 1890 and 2007 Pittsburg incidents demonstrate, tornado history can repeat itself.

On the same day that Pittsburg was hit in 1884, a tornado notable for the severity of its damage struck Colemansville, a small Harrison County community located a mile west of Berry's Station. Initial reports claimed that eight were killed and ten wounded, but it was later discovered that the only fatality was a three-week-old baby of the

Albert Lail family who was yanked from its mother's arms and dashed against a tree a hundred yards away. Only two of the roughly twenty houses in town were not totally destroyed. The tornado denuded several trees of their bark and carried the organ in the Colemansville Baptist Church three hundred yards.

Winter tornados are rare, but one of the fiercest in Kentucky history struck Clinton, Hickman County, and Wickliffe, Ballard County, on January 12, 1890—an unseasonably warm Sunday. It originated in Sardis, Mississippi, and traveled up through Tennessee, Kentucky, Illinois and Missouri. North of New Madrid, Missouri, it crossed the river—proving that, contrary to popular belief, a tornado *will* cross a large body of water if it takes a mind to—flattened several buildings at Moscow, Kentucky, and moved on to Clinton, arriving at about 6:00 p.m. At Clinton, witnesses noticed, as happens often before a tornado, that the city experienced only a moderate storm at first; then a period of stillness; and then the cyclone came boiling into the east end of town. An eloquent witness described it as "the most curious thing that ever came before my range of vision":

> *Imagine a cloud black as tar, whirling around like mad, and shooting up, down and athwart this pitchy mass were millions of sparks or balls of fire that moved with lightning-like rapidity. The nearest simile I can make is to compare the effect to that of a great shower of sparks and flying embers that have sprung with a mighty wave from a burning building, whose massive walls have crumbled and fallen in upon the fiery furnace. Accompanying all this was the most dreadful sound I ever heard: a roaring, thundering, rumbling, quaking noise, that could only be likened to the sound of the rolling of a hundred trains of cars… Everybody who happened to be upon the streets felt in their bones that something terrible was about to take place, and that something did occur.*

Indeed it did. People ran into their houses to close their doors and shutters, actions that we now know to be ineffective, time wasting and dangerous. It was all over within fifteen minutes. Rescuers grabbed axes, saws and levers and hurried to Clinton's stricken district, where they could hear the cries of the wounded and the trapped over the sound of the pounding rain. The debris showed that the tornado was three hundred yards wide; it destroyed fifty-five houses and injured fifty-three persons, of whom eight were said to be fatally hurt. The tornado did an estimated

$100,000 worth of property damage, but the lives of at least ten citizens were an incalculable loss. An eyewitness report stated, "For several miles around Clinton nearly everything is razed to the ground." If this was accurate, ten dead was a very small toll under the circumstances. Immediately after the tornado passed, the weather became wintry cold, and a sleet shower added to the injuries of the miserable victims.

Strange and tragic stories emerge after a storm of such violence. A two-year-old girl was carried two hundred feet by the wind and dropped in a pond; she nearly drowned. According to one report, "The infant child of [John] Gaddie, the merchant, was found in its dead father's arms asleep and unharmed." (A second conflicting account states that the child died as well, and a third asserts that Mr. Gaddie was injured but not killed.) The lower floor of Robert Johnson's two-story house was knocked away, leaving the upper floor to crash down onto the foundation unscathed and leaving the structure looking as though it had always had one story. Reportedly, the furniture on the upper—now the first—floor was not even disturbed, although falling timbers injured Johnson and his sons, Robert and Dave. The house of Mr. Gwynne was lifted, carried one hundred feet and dropped in Judge W.F. Boone's yard. The wife and son of another townsman, W.D. Boone, were killed when their residence took a direct hit; the boy was found two hundred yards from the house with the back of his head missing. A house belonging to a woman named Taylor was lifted intact from its foundation and moved elsewhere.

Dave Stubblefield's family was saved when they instinctively did something recommended by modern meteorologists: they took shelter in an inner hallway. Their house was destroyed entirely—except for one wall that protected the hallway.

Of the five members of the John Rhodes family, the father and three children were killed outright, and Mrs. Rhodes was fatally hurt.

When the tornado hit the brand-new two-story residence of James R. Graham, twelve of the thirteen family members were injured. One daughter, Mattie, had been playing the piano when the house exploded; she had a missing scalp and a "broken limb," to use the fussy language of the era. Despite her pain, she insisted that rescuers pick her brother Jimmy out of the rubble first. Mrs. Graham and three other family members died of their injuries within a week.

The storm's fury was hardly spent when it left Clinton. Wickliffe was luckier than its neighboring town—if having eight persons injured

A nineteenth-century newspaper artist's rendering of a tornado striking a city. *Louisville Courier-Journal*, April 6, 1890. *Courtesy of the* Courier-Journal.

and thirteen houses destroyed can be considered lucky. No one was killed, which is remarkable considering that the tornado had enough force to lift five loaded Illinois Central freight cars off the train track and throw them against the depot. After striking Wickliffe, it went to St. Louis, where it still packed enough punch to uproot trees, unroof buildings, severely damage structures—including toppling a ninety-foot brewery smokestack—and injure a number of people. (I cannot resist including the story of Mr. Verfield, who was injured when the tornado destroyed the doors of the St. Louis Manufacturing Company as a preamble and then blew him inside the building and threw him down the stairs.) On January 12 and 13, violent storms also struck Chicago, Cleveland, Toledo, Cincinnati, Detroit, Pittsburgh, Buffalo, Syracuse and Rochester, with authentic tornados striking Niagara Falls and at least two Illinois towns: Cooksville, where the temperature fell fifty degrees between midnight and sunrise; and Machburg, where dead birds allegedly were found stripped of their feathers. But at least the weather was nice and summery in Delaware.

Those are a few of the significant pre-1890 tornados endured by the Bluegrass State in general. Now we come to consider Louisville exclusively. The city has never been immune from tornados; its history is replete with many near-misses and minor hits. About 1830, for example, a tornado crossed the Ohio River above Louisville. Only six miles separated the city from the cyclone. The harmless event was repeated about ten years later.

In 1835, a tornado strolled through the city, taking a path almost identical to the route that the killer tornado of 1890 would take fifty-five years later. It came from the southwest across fields that later would become the suburb of Parkland, cut a northeasterly swath through town and toured the waterfront. Louisville was still a relatively small city with a population of fifteen thousand, so while the tornado destroyed property, no lives were lost.

The most devastating tornado that Louisville had ever faced—for a few decades, at least—occurred on August 27, 1854. It struck a Presbyterian church at the corner of Eleventh and Walnut Streets during Sunday morning services, killing eighteen people. "The bodies of those who had perished were, in most instances, badly mangled," a writer recalled decades later, "and as they were carried from the stricken building and recognized, the cries of their friends and relatives were heart-rending." The tornado destroyed a number of buildings and dislodged several steamboats and barges from their moorings, but the only fatalities were at the church.

On May 21, 1860, a monster tornado traveled from Louisville to Portsmouth, Ohio, wreaking prodigious havoc in the countryside and killing one hundred people. According to historian Richard Collins, the *Louisville Courier* and the *Cincinnati Gazette*, the tornado traveled 245 miles and left a damage path 40 miles wide; this is impossible to believe, since the most powerful American cyclone in recorded history was the Tri-State Tornado of March 18, 1925, which traveled 219 miles across Missouri, Illinois and Indiana and was estimated to be 1 mile wide at the broadest. Embellishment aside, the 1860 storm was devastating. Unlike most tornados that strike only part of a city, if press reports do not exaggerate, this one gave the entire city a comprehensive battering. A *Courier* reporter wrote, "Although the storm was of short duration, it was destructive in the extreme, extending all over the city." (We should take into account the fact that the city covered a much smaller area then.) While Louisville saw severe property damage and a number of injuries, there were only two fatalities, both workmen killed by a falling building at the corner of Fourteenth Street and Portland Avenue. Other cities fared far, far worse, including the Indiana cities of Jeffersonville, New Albany and Madison, and Cincinnati, which alone received $1 million worth of damage—an astronomical sum in 1860.

An especially nightmarish scenario unfolded in Louisville on the night of March 10, 1873, when tornadic winds snapped in half the main supporting pole of the Great Eastern circus tent—with seven thousand spectators under it. Several were injured in the ensuing panic, and two boys were killed. Had the tigers, panthers, lions, hairy-nosed wombats and other exotic animals escaped from their cages, and had the lamps not been extinguished, things certainly would have taken a much worse turn. The circus gave the proceeds of its March 12 benefit performance, a total of $585, to the families of the victims.

On May 27 of the same year, a tornado passed over Louisville but did nothing worse than lift roofs, crumble chimneys and topple trees.

In the pre-dawn hours of November 28, 1879, the southwestern section of the city was visited by a tornado that destroyed fences, uprooted trees and did severe damage to houses. No one was badly injured except a man named Mike Hermann, who was pinned under a collapsing wall in his cottage on Mechanic Street. The night before the storm, Hermann's sister had rearranged her bed so that it would face her clock; had she not done so, she likely would have been killed because a load of bricks landed in the spot where her bed had stood. Witnesses saw a rotating cloud, so the storm was a genuine tornado and not merely a severe thunderstorm. It must have been a frightening spectacle. "The sight was an awful one," wrote a *Courier-Journal* reporter, "and calculated to make those who had not been duly thankful the day before repentant for their shortcomings."

Despite these sporadic warnings from Mother Nature, Louisvillians in 1890 were not particularly worried about tornados. After all, the 1854 storm was the last such event in which there had been significant loss of life—and that had been thirty-six years before. Besides, it was thought that the city's location made it relatively safe. Louisville had a sizable waterfront, and "everyone knew" that tornados won't cross large bodies of water. Also, as a *Courier-Journal* reporter wrote in May 1886, "Louisville…is so protected by the high hills across the river that storms are very uncommon, and cyclones almost unknown." In the same year, a Louisville insurance agent estimated that he had issued only thirty-two policies against damage caused by tornados. Louisville was so complacent that only five insurance companies in the city even offered such coverage.

The general feeling that the city was not susceptible to tornados was described in 1938 by former Seventh Street resident John Doyle:

No one had the least thought of a cyclone. I doubt if any one of us had a real conception of the meaning of the word. We had always been told that Louisville was immune from disasters of any and every kind. A cyclone could not find entry into Louisville because the Indiana Knobs protected us, and there was no place of entry for a cyclone to penetrate.

Then came Thursday, March 27, 1890.

The storm front that created disaster for Louisville originated around Leavenworth, Kansas. Early that morning, the United States Signal Corps warned Sergeant Frank Burke at its Louisville office to keep an eye out for violent storms in the next twenty-four hours. Burke noticed that the barometer fell steadily, which meant that bad weather was brewing. All day long, the Signal Corps received messages from other offices located along the storm's route that an uncommonly fierce front was heading its way. Having received this news, Sergeant Burke placed at least one telephone call, evidently to the officials at the city's waterfront, to be on the lookout for a tornado. Only one man heeded the warning: Captain John Kirker of the steamer *City of Madison*, who built up full steam in his vessel just in case it should be necessary later. At 1:30 p.m., the Signal Corps office in Washington, D.C., issued a bulletin describing the origin and progress of the storm and warning the states of Ohio, Indiana, Illinois, Tennessee, Kentucky, Georgia and Alabama to be cautious. However, it did not mention specific locales—such as Louisville.

That spring evening was much like any other in the big city. The weather forecast printed in the morning *Courier-Journal*—which of course went to press before the Signal Corps received updated information—was not ominous: "The indications for today in Kentucky are fair weather, followed in western portion by rain, easterly winds, and stationary temperature." The *Times*, an afternoon paper, did publish a warning; however, the writer had no idea of the magnitude of the storm that was on the way.

The most excitement the city anticipated was fear that recent heavy rains might cause a dam to burst; residents of the section known as "the Point" were loading their wagons and fleeing the neighborhood. On the other hand, citizens were relieved to hear that high water in the Ohio was falling rapidly, easing concerns that the city might face another devastating flood like the one in February 1884.

In other news, the mourners at Judge W.L. Jackson's funeral in Cave Hill Cemetery were drenched in a driving rain that day. The city fathers were trying to decide on a good location for the Louisville Fair. Local brick makers and bricklayers were on strike; before the end of the day, their wares and services would be in great, though unexpected, demand.

The majority of citizens were concerned neither with the rain, the strike nor the shaky dam at the Point. The day's work was done, and it was time to relax. Some workers sought refuge at home with their families; some went to saloons; some simply wanted to be entertained. And there was plenty of entertainment for the masses. Highbrow folk could go to Macauley's Theatre in the afternoon for a concert devoted to Schumann, advertised as being "a composer little known except to professional musicians." Those with middlebrow tastes could attend H.H. Ragan's illustrated lecture on the topic of "Picturesque Ireland," also at Macauley's. For everybody else, there was the option of seeing Professor D.M. Bristol's educated horses, mules and ponies at the Masonic Temple Theatre. Many Louisvillians, craving the society of others or seeking self-improvement, went to the Falls City Hall to attend lodge meetings or take dancing lessons.

In short, all was as usual in Louisville until about 7:00 p.m., when the barometer reading at the Signal Corps office was a low 29.274 inches. The drop in atmospheric pressure came so swiftly that gaslights went out all over the city. A severe rainstorm came, followed by hail averaging a half inch in diameter. The temperature was fifty degrees; abruptly, it rose to sixty-eight. Many years later, in 1962, Hazel Miller of Somerset, Pulaski County, described the weather conditions before this most memorable storm from her youth. She remembered the heat of the day and the rain and hail that fell just before the tornado. She also remembered that "a peculiar stillness occurred as a magnificent electrical display stabbed the intense darkness. The smell of brimstone was in the air."

About 7:45 p.m., a powerful five-minute gale worked plenty of damage on its own. After that came another windstorm, also of five minutes' duration. The purple prose of a *Courier-Journal* reporter described these fierce winds as fighting "impatiently to accomplish the work reserved for the whirling tiger of the air, whose avant couriers they were." These winds destroyed the city's telegraph lines, so the Signal Corps was unable to warn of the imminent peril. After the

The tornado gets its work in on Louisville. *Louisville Courier-Journal*, April 6, 1890. *Courtesy of the* Courier-Journal.

two terrifying wind gusts were over, Louisvillians came out of hiding, thinking that the worst was over. There was a brief respite of calm. Owing to the unreliability of the era's clocks, accounts vary as to exactly when the disaster struck, but between 8:00 and 8:30 p.m., the city was given an unforgettable visit by the so-called "whirling tiger of the air."

PART II

During

The tornado approached Louisville from the southwest at thirty-six to forty miles per hour, as later estimated by Sergeant Burke of the Signal Corps; it sounded, said Burke, like "the passage of a heavy train of cars over a bridge, 1,000 times intensified." It started as a relatively small but destructive cyclone when it passed through the Parkland suburb, traveling in a northeastwardly diagonal path. It entered the city limits at Scott Grove and leveled houses on the north side of Garland Avenue, the first street in Louisville to face the storm's wrath. The tornado's early stage was witnessed by E.X. Jackman of Garland Avenue, who described it as being full of "yellowish flames," probably lightning, from bottom to top. It was so brilliantly illuminated that Jackman thought at first that lightning had destroyed the grove and nearby houses. (Years later, Hazel Miller also remembered that "lightning played on the ground like balls of fire.")

The tornado at this point was only seventy-five yards wide and also inflicted a twenty-five-yard margin of partial, as opposed to total, destruction. Others who saw the tornado that night remembered that it was shaped like a balloon or a turnip rather than the canonical funnel. Strangely, the highest wind velocity measured by the Signal Corps office that night was a mere thirty-six miles per hour, despite the fact that the tornado passed within six hundred yards of the office. Considering the spectacular damage wrought by the winds, we can assume that the low reading was due to faulty equipment.

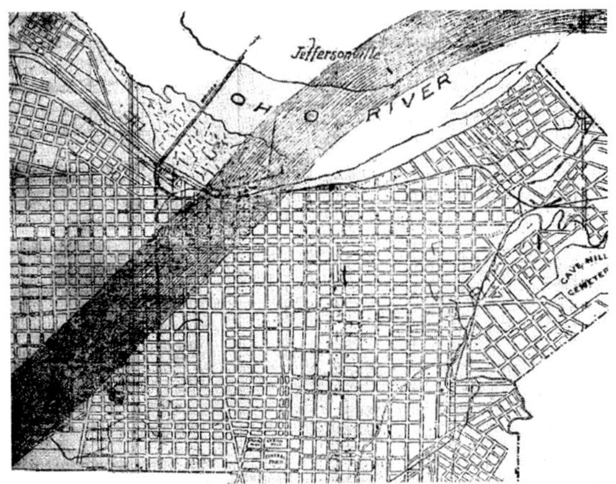

Map showing the tornado's path through the city, across the Ohio River and on to Jeffersonville, Indiana. *Louisville Courier-Journal*, April 6, 1890. *Courtesy of the* Courier-Journal.

After hitting Garland Avenue, the tornado bounced over five blocks and entered the city proper at Eighteenth and Maple Streets, striking the important streets of Broadway, Magazine, Chestnut, Madison, Walnut (now Muhammad Ali Boulevard), Grayson, Jefferson, Market and Main, in that order, and also many smaller streets that intersected with these major thoroughfares.

Houses were wrecked along Maple Street, especially on the western side. At the northeast corner of Eighteenth and Maple, the tornado claimed its first victims. John Emerich, his wife and their nine children lived in a low two-story frame house constructed of subpar material. He operated a grocery and saloon on the ground floor and lived with his family on the second story. When the tornado struck, the only people in the saloon were Emerich and Fred Depp, a fireman on the C&O Railroad. The building fell "like a house of cards," burying the proprietor and his customer. The rest of the family had been on the second floor; some managed to escape, but others were pinned down by timbers. Neighbors came to the rescue despite the darkness and the driving rain, but exposed gas mains caught fire, and soon the debris was burning. Men dug frantically and thought they had rescued Mrs. Emerich and all of her children. After the fire was extinguished, excavators found the body of Mr. Emerich with a crushed head; it was thought that he was the only victim, so workers sought other places where their help was needed.

In the morning light, however, observers saw a small hand protruding from the wreckage. Digging revealed the body of Emerich's four-year-old daughter, Emma. All through the night, a nervous young woman had stood at the gate of a cottage across the street. "I believe that my brother

The storm's first victims: John Emerich and his small daughter Emma. *Louisville Courier-Journal*, April 6, 1890. *Courtesy of the* Courier-Journal.

is killed in that house over there," she told a reporter as she pointed to the ruins of the Emerich house. She was Fred Depp's sister, and exploration of the wreckage proved her fears correct.

From Eighteenth and Maple, the storm moved onto Broadway, which escaped serious damage, but the section that fell between Fifteenth and Nineteenth Streets was "a perfect wreck." Schools, residences, saloons, a barbershop and other places of business were flattened.

The most significant harm befell the Church of the Sacred Heart at the northeast corner of Seventeenth and Broadway, as well as the church's school, rectory and convent. The church and its adjoining buildings were demolished in seconds despite their solid brick construction. Several nuns in the convent chapel escaped through the rear exit as the tornado hit, but Sister Mary Pius was crushed under a wall as she made her evening devotions before a statue of the Virgin Mary.

After the tornado passed, nothing stood undamaged on the church's property except the statue of the Virgin Mary, which suffered only a missing fingertip. The $25,000 church had been completed only five years before under the auspices of Father T.J. Disney. It had been his life's work; a *Courier-Journal* report mentioned the melancholy sight of the Father staring with tears in his eyes as he contemplated "all that remained of years of labor and self-denial."

After killing Sister Mary Pius and demolishing Father Disney's church, the tornado entered Magazine Street at Sixteenth. On Magazine, virtually everything was destroyed on the two blocks between Fifteenth and Seventeenth Streets. Most of the residents in this area were poor and felt their losses bitterly. The most horrifying event on the street befell customers at a grocery and saloon owned by John Thierman (variously spelled Thieneman, Tiernan and Tierney in news accounts), located on the northeast corner of Sixteenth Street and Magazine. Five men were in the bar when the storm hit: proprietor Thierman; his brother, Nick; Thierman's brother-in-law, undertaker Ben Schildt; and Nick Sullivan and William Diemer, both employees of the Pullman Car Company. In seconds, saloonkeeper and customers were buried under fallen timbers. John and Nick Thierman managed to get free, but the other three were trapped. The wreckage caught fire. By the time the fire department made it to the scene, it was too late. All the firefighters could do was pull the charred bodies of Schildt, Sullivan and Diemer out of the smoldering ruins and place them beside one another on the sidewalk. Nick Sullivan's elderly father was unable to identify which was his son. The three were distinguished by their watches and other pieces of jewelry.

Chestnut Street was described as being one of the most beautiful portions of the city—until the twister left Magazine and entered Chestnut at Sixteenth. The tornado appears to have been still forming, since its path was only three-fourths of a block wide. As an illustration of the capriciousness of a tornado's winds, on the north side of Chestnut Street for three blocks all houses but six were damaged; on the south side of the street, all houses but six were left relatively unharmed. On the other hand, the trees on the north side of the street were left untouched, while trees on the south side were yanked up by the roots. Despite the destruction of the Third Presbyterian Church and a number of houses, there were no fatalities on Chestnut Street.

The track of the tornado's damage on Madison Street stretched from Eleventh to Fourteenth Street. Every house in the district was damaged to some extent, but nobody was fatally injured. The residents of the next street would not be so fortunate.

Most of the damage on Walnut Street was confined to the blocks between Twelfth and Fourteenth Streets. Only the houses on the north side of the street were destroyed. Dr. F.W. Muguet and his wife were injured when their house at 1319 Walnut was crushed "like an egg shell." The second floor of the neighboring house came crashing into the room in which they were sitting. The Muguets were rescued after spending several uncomfortable hours buried in the wreckage, but they had to wait several additional hours for medical attention.

The tornado struck Eclipse Hall at 1230 Walnut, where the Adam Lodge of the black chapter of the Odd Fellows fraternal order was meeting. Fifteen members were present; they had gotten as far as the reading of

Ruins of Eclipse Hall. *Wilburn Stereographs; 99.36.026; Special Collections, University of Louisville.*

the minutes of the previous meeting when the building began trembling. The windows and walls facing Walnut Street actually bulged inwardly. The men ran for the door—which, unfortunately, they had locked since the meetings of the society were supposed to be kept secret. A moment later, all was crumbling building, collapsing floor, tumbling lodge members and lightning flashes that illuminated the scene. The members were trapped under debris, afraid that their lodge's coal stove would set the building on fire. The earliest news reports state that a fire did break out, burning the men alive. However, later accounts confirm that while eight lodge members were hurt, none was killed. After they spent ten worrisome minutes praying under the debris, a strong gust of wind shifted the position of the collapsed roof, allowing the men to crawl out, injured but alive. Their survival was called marvelous, considering the damage wrought upon the building: its two upper floors were gone, and the remaining floor had large circular holes in the brick walls. The lodge members had been saved by large wooden chests that partially supported the debris. "The destruction of this building is particularly unfortunate to the Colored Odd Fellows order of this city who purchased it five or six years ago [for $10,000]," remarked a *Courier-Journal* reporter a couple of days after the tornado. "They have made a heroic struggle to pay for it, and only $2,000 of the purchase money remained unpaid." The building was demolished beyond repair, at an estimated loss of $10,000 (modern equivalent of $235,000).

An order for black women, the Lancaster Lodge of Daughters of Samaria, was in session on the third floor of Eclipse Hall. Fortunately, few members were present, the nasty weather preceding the tornado having encouraged most to stay at home. As they waited for other lodge sisters to arrive—the initiation of Mrs. Charity Duly being the major item of business—the tornado hit. Kittie Trotter recalled that the wind lifted the carpet up from the floor. She ran to get her pocketbook; the next thing she knew, she had been struck by a flying window. When lightning flashed, she could see another woman hanging from the eaves of the building. Mrs. Trotter—who, I can't resist adding, was also the princess of another lodge intriguingly named Sisters of the Mysterious Ten—attempted to follow the woman outside when the floor collapsed, sending her crashing down to the first floor and breaking her leg. She beseeched a terrified male passerby for help; he dragged her roughly through the mud across the street to a German tailor's shop, tearing off most of her dress in the process. By the time he let go of her, she was not wearing enough clothing to wad a shotgun. On the other hand, said Mrs. Trotter, "The German people were very good to me. They sent for a doctor who bandaged my leg." She never did manage to get her pocketbook. The other members of the Daughters of Samaria, like their counterparts in the Adam Lodge of Odd Fellows, received an impressive array of injuries, but none was killed. One who was not present, Amanda Lancaster, was delayed because she had stopped by the house of a sick member to check on her health. When she made it to Walnut Street, she found Eclipse Hall in ruins.

Only one person died on Walnut Street: Moody Davis, who was at first erroneously reported to have been a member of the Odd Fellows lodge. He was impaled as he crossed the street at Thirteenth and Walnut. A

March 29 *Courier-Journal* article described Moody Davis's untimely end in baroque detail: "A large, pointed rafter, which had been torn from the roof of a neighboring building, pierced him just below the right shoulder and, passing clear through his body, came out just above his right hip, killing him instantly. He was picked up by trembling hands and borne to his home on Magazine Street."

The tornado moved onto Grayson Street, where it destroyed many houses and buildings but killed no one. It may even have temporarily weakened. But afterward, it rallied and seemed to grow stronger and gain momentum with every street it crossed. (In 1938, John Doyle remembered that he followed the path of the tornado through the city and noticed that the damage increased the farther he traveled.) When it roared up Thirteenth Street, it did little more than lift some tin roofs; by the time it reached Twelfth and the major thoroughfare of Jefferson Street, it had gained significantly in power and leveled every house on the northeast corner except two. The homes of F.J. Clark and his neighbor E.M. Gibbs were both demolished—nothing remained of the Clark house but one standing wall—yet somehow all members of both families escaped injury. Beside their houses was the residence of Dr. George Griffiths. The doctor and his wife were out of the state, but their six children, several of their friends and Dr. Patton Griffiths were home. Despite the fact that the physician's house and adjoining office were shaved level to the ground, all the occupants were thrown unharmed into the yard. They were joined a moment later by James Lee, who was thrown from a second-story window of a neighboring house. The house next to that was occupied by the family of Reverend Stephen Barnwell, formerly a Confederate soldier from South Carolina and currently the rector of St. John's Episcopal Church on Jefferson Street, who was widely beloved for his saintliness and jolly personality.

St. John's Episcopal Church, where the Barnwells died. *Louisville Courier-Journal*, March 29, 1890. *Courtesy of the* Courier-Journal.

St. John's. Note the signs painted on the church reading "Danger" and "Keep Out." *Wilburn Stereographs; 99.36.005; Special Collections, University of Louisville.*

The Barnwells were at home reading when the church and rectory were hit; nothing remained of the former but the façade, belfry and pulpit, in which stood a tall, unharmed brass cross. The rectory virtually disintegrated. A *Courier-Journal* reporter described the result in language not calculated to bring comfort to Mrs. Barnwell:

> [F]*rom his position when found,* [Reverend Barnwell] *must have been killed instantly. His head was horribly crushed, his chest caved in, and his whole body bruised and mangled almost beyond recognition. His beautiful boy, who was evidently sitting at his father's knee, was killed by a terrible fracture of the skull, and was also torn and mangled.*

The reporter added that the reverend's face was "horribly expressive of the terrible agony which for an instant he must have suffered in the knowledge of the direful death that was upon him." Mrs. Barnwell and two other children were taken from the ruins badly injured; the doctor gave orders that the catatonic and heavily sedated Mrs. Barnwell not be told yet of her husband's and son's fates, so let's hope that neighbors kept that *Courier-Journal* article away from her.

As the tornado moved up Jefferson Street, it obstructed the street in some sections with roofs from destroyed buildings that had been thrown as far as three blocks. At Baxter Square, Louisville's first public park, located across from the ruined rectory, enormous century-old oak trees were uprooted and thrown into the street; the iron fence around the square was pulled out of its stone foundation. The park's beautiful statues, music pavilion and bridges were destroyed; in some places, these materials were buried several feet in the ground. More than a week after the storm passed, Baxter Square—which had been in existence for only a decade—was described as still being "a network of wires and treetops," in the center of which roosted the unclaimed roof from some building.

Oddly, Green Street, located near Baxter Square, got off with only unroofed houses, crumbled chimneys and broken windows. The only utterly destroyed buildings were Mary McKenne's three-story house and the old Green Street police station.

Market Street, the next hit, received the most severe harm and suffered the greatest loss of life, especially on the north side of the street. Every house between Seventh and Twelfth Streets sustained some damage; every house between Ninth and Eleventh was demolished. Several loafers outside Frank Eckerle's bar at 1001 West Market saw the tornado coming and rushed inside. Within seconds, everyone was in the cellar, accompanied by broken pieces of the saloon. Elmer Barnes's throat was cut "from ear to ear" by a piece of flying glass, and he died several hours later. The other men escaped death. Eckerle survived despite being so badly wounded that it was thought he would die. (Some people seem marked by fate to undergo unpleasant adventures. Fourteen years later, Eckerle would find the freshly murdered body of Fannie Porter in an upstairs room in his second saloon, as recounted in my book *Offbeat Kentuckians*.)

G.W. Becker was tending to business in his West Market Street grocery; outside stood Policeman Harlow, Charles Taylor, an unknown man and an eight-year-old boy named Carl Rice. Suddenly, a powerful

Market Street between Tenth and Eleventh. *Wilburn Stereographs; 99.36.006; Special Collections, University of Louisville.*

wind howled up the street, and hail showered from the heavens. Officer Harlow tried to push open Becker's door, but the force of the wind kept it from budging—even when Becker's clerk pulled on the opposite side of the door. Then, the tornado sent the upper floor of the store crashing down onto the pavement where the onlookers had been standing. Harlow and the little boy sustained minor wounds, but Taylor received a broken leg and internal injuries, and the unknown man received a hole in his head "larger than a silver dollar." The man was later carried away for treatment, but the unnerved storekeeper hung his muddy, bloody hat on a post on the edge of the sidewalk. "No one disturbed it after it was hung on the post," wrote a reporter three days after the event, "and there it still hangs, a sad and gory reminder of that awful night."

The Falls City Hall, located at 1126 Market Street between Eleventh and Twelfth Streets, was the most tragic scene in Louisville that night. The

Ruins of Falls City Hall as depicted in an unknown contemporary magazine. *From the Keven McQueen accumulation.*

structure had been built in 1871 and was popularly used for lodge meetings and classes. Several such meetings were being held on the night of March 27. The building suffered a direct hit so powerful that much of it was pushed into Market Street. In the lower rooms, between 50 and 75 children—no one could say exactly how many—and many parents were attending a dancing class taught by Miss Rosa App (called Annie). By 8:00 p.m., the class was over, but many chose to remain in the sturdy building until the inclement weather passed. On the second floor, 7 members of the executive committee of the Roman Knights fraternity were in session. On the third floor, the Humboldt Lodge of the International Order of Odd Fellows and the Jewel Lodge of the Knights and Ladies of Honor—an estimated 150 souls, two-thirds of them women, including visitors and children—were holding a meeting. When the building commenced shaking, some people leaped from the windows and survived. The second and third floors collapsed, but the wall facing Market Street remained standing and sheltered some of the dancing school attendees.

An officer of the Knights and Ladies of Honor later remembered that he was speaking to an elderly member, James Stephens, when a large crack appeared in the shaking building. As panicking people headed for the exit, there was a rain of debris and then utter blackness. Moments later, the officer was standing outside surrounded by ruins as the moonlight shone down upon him. The secretary of the lodge still sat stunned at a table with his record book open before him.

In a matter of seconds, Falls City Hall was a pile of rubble from which issued the cries of scores of injured or dying people. Owing to the whimsical disposition of the tornado, the houses on either side of the doomed building sustained only cracked walls.

The tornado then moved on to the area between Tenth and Eleventh Streets. Property damage was even more fearsome here, but while a number of people were wounded, no one was killed. There were some close calls: four children of shopkeeper Isaac Slaughter were protected from a falling wall by their bed's headboard, which no doubt became a prized family keepsake. Their mother was lifted from her bed and sucked through a window. She landed in the middle of the street with a broken arm. Mattie Nelson, a clothing merchant's servant girl, fell through a second-story window and slid safely to the ground on a post.

The tornado went from Market to Main Street, the commercial center of Louisville. The cyclone had been widening in size as it traveled and was at its broadest on Main, where it covered eight hundred yards (or about five blocks). It hit particularly hard between Eighth and Thirteenth Streets. Virtually every house was unroofed between Seventh and Eighth Streets—and those were the fortunate ones. Others were destroyed wholly or partially. Two four-story buildings—Whalen's blacksmith shop and the Carpenter-Annear Galvanized Ironworks—were reduced to piles of bricks. Brown and Son's five-story whisky house was bereft of its entire front and was also burned when its store of alcohol caught fire. The building of another liquor retailer, H.A. Thierman, had its two top floors removed and its stock destroyed by falling bricks and plaster. The tobacco storage warehouse west of Sixth Street, recently built by the Sawyer-Wallace Company, was rendered an unrecognizable ruin. Louisville's entire tobacco district was destroyed; only three of fourteen warehouses were left standing. Charles Jenks was killed when the roof of a warehouse collapsed on him. His watch was still ticking when his body was recovered. A.B. Burnham and Co.'s hardware and stove store was flattened; the shoe sellers Bamberger, Streng, and Co. lost their roof and fourth floor; and the third and fourth floors of F.W. Johanbocke's hat and cap store collapsed onto the second floor. (After the storm, some merchants displayed fine gallows humor by placing signs on what was left of their stores informing customers that their businesses had "moved to a new location.")

These were just a few of the many business casualties in the Main Street area. Most of these establishments were closed at the time of the disaster, the tornado having struck in the evening. However, Charles Rosenheim's queensware store, located at 746 Main Street, was open, and several salesmen and customers were injured by falling wreckage when the roof flew off. Salesman Charles Bainrod had been filling

Planters' Warehouse, scene of two workers' deaths. Note the man hauling building materials in the foreground. *Wilburn Stereographs; 99.36.043; Special Collections, University of Louisville.*

out an order form for customer H.M. Blackburn. Bainrod was able to walk home, but Blackburn bled internally. In addition, rescuers found a man, who gave his name only as Robinson, pinned under a wall. Despite his severe injuries, Robinson got to his feet and staggered off into the night.

The worst destruction on Main Street occurred at number 640, a building adjoining the Louisville Hotel and occupied chiefly by cigar impresario Virgil Wright but also by saloonkeeper Ike Baer and ticket-broker J.P. McFarland. A number of laundresses who worked next door at the hotel took their lodgings in the upper floor of Wright's store. The tornado's winds caused a large piece of the hotel to fall on number 640.

Barroom patrons were crushed alongside several laundresses, whose apartment was pitched into the building's basement. Survivors recalled that the women's screams could be heard even above the roar of the storm and the crumbling building. Afterward, the voices of trapped laundresses

Main Street between Eighth and Ninth. *Wilburn Stereographs; 99.36.034; Special Collections, University of Louisville.*

issued from the wreckage, encouraging rescuers to dig them out. Help came too late for five women: Maggie Campbell, Bridget Crowe, Katie McCue, Mary McGinty and Mary Ryan—Irish immigrants, judging from their names. (Campbell, the hotel's chief laundress, had been employed there for twenty-five years.) Virgil Wright was found barely alive in a corner under a pile of bricks and mortar. He was armed with a pistol, and rescuers found him trying to put himself out of his misery. He was too injured to pull the trigger. In short order, the workmen found the gruesomely crushed bodies of bartender Frank Paul; Thaddeus Mason of Nashville, who had recently moved to Louisville; C.H. Hathaway, a traveling salesman from Chicago; Fritz Delph; and Alexander R. McKee from Mercer County, Danville in Boyle County or Richmond in Madison County (accounts differ, but most likely he was from Boyle County since that is where he was shipped for burial). For some reason, Delph's name doesn't turn up in the early accounts of the disaster at Wright's store, but the revised death list in the April 2 *Courier-Journal* confirms that he lost his life there.

Virgil Wright's store, crushed by a piece of the Louisville Hotel. *Louisville Courier-Journal*, April 6, 1890. *Courtesy of the* Courier-Journal.

Two Catholic priests, "with that splendid heroism that characterizes their profession," as the *Courier-Journal* complimented them, came to administer rites for the dying and the dead in spite of the danger posed by fire and precariously balanced rubble. In all, ten men and women were killed in Wright's store; the Louisville Hotel would pay for the funerals of its laundresses. Two laundresses, Mary Crowe and Mary Farrell, and two customers, Joseph McFarland and Edward Minter, barely escaped. Considering the ferocity of the tornado by the time it reached Main Street, it is amazing that the only casualties there were the ones at Wright's store.

After wreaking havoc on Main Street, the tornado approached the riverfront. One of the most spectacular ruins in this section of Louisville was the Union Depot at the foot of Seventh Street, the debris from which blocked the city's elevated railway. About fifty people were in the building waiting for trains. Unlike others in the city for whom the tornado came as a surprise, the depot was far enough away from the point of touchdown that the commuters had plenty of time to hear it coming. Despite this warning, rather than flee the building or seek shelter, the people in the depot huddled and awaited the inevitable: the tornado lifted the depot an estimated three feet in the air and moved it several feet north. People a half-dozen blocks away heard the crash. (Contrary to later rumor, the building was not dropped bodily into the river.) By a stroke of fate, the train cars in the depot supported much of the debris. Twenty men were buried in the debris, a dozen of whom were seriously hurt but none killed.

The Louisville Southern train from Harrodsburg and Lexington had arrived just before the tornado hit. The roof collapsed on the emerging passengers as they walked through the gates leading to the street; no one was injured, but two horses were so badly hurt that they had to be shot. Miraculously, passengers sitting aboard the Cincinnati-bound train also

Union Depot. *Wilburn Stereographs; 99.36.009; Special Collections, University of Louisville.*

escaped unscathed. The only known human fatality at the depot was William Geissel, a boy who operated a newsstand.

The city's general council was in session at city hall at an inconvenient time, and Louisville's movers and shakers did plenty of moving and shaking when they heard the roar of the tornado, followed by exploding windows. It was an opportune time to introduce new legislation outlawing tornados within city limits, but instead the politicians headed outside or for the basement. Although the building was hardly damaged, a reporter noted that "everyone was in a state of terror, and when the storm had subsided it was all that could be done to get the Councilmen and Aldermen to return to their seats." Hardly had they done so when they got word that sections of the city were on fire. They felt they could not work under such circumstances, and the meeting was adjourned.

The tornado did so much creative damage to streetcars that one is tempted to consider them the mobile homes of their day. On Eighteenth Street, a streetcar was lifted by the wind and brought to earth upside-down. The driver managed to escape uninjured. On Market Street, another streetcar was picked up off its tracks and thrown fifteen feet into the side of Mrs. Cohen's clothing and shoe store. The driver received a broken arm and leg. Another driver was seriously injured when he was struck by the tin roof of Rubel Brothers' lithographing shop below Seventh Street on Main. A streetcar on Main Street, between Eighth and Ninth, was flung from its track and halfway through the wall of a tobacco warehouse. The driver and the sole occupant, a young woman, were killed.

Sailors on the waterfront heard a low moaning sound from the southwest that got louder until it sounded like a train barreling down upon them. A howling wind seemed to come from Third Street and the Commercial Club Building simultaneously. Men on steamboats, barges, tugboats and smaller craft were suddenly confronted with waves that seemed the size of mountains. Chains and restraining ropes snapped, and several ships were beaten together, swept into the river and carried away by the current. Captain John Kirker of the *City of Madison*—who had been warned by the Signal Corps that a tornado was likely and who had built up full steam in case of an emergency—followed the smashed ships. The men aboard the crippled vessels threw ropes toward his boat. The lines were tied, and the *City of Madison* slowly towed them all ashore. The crew of the *Madison* was responsible for saving the lives of sailors who otherwise may have been swept over the waterfalls. Captain Devan and his men aboard the *Ready* showed similar heroism when they saw a powerless steamboat, the *Hibernia*, drifting by with its terror-stricken crew clinging to the roof. After precarious feats of derring-do, Devan's men managed to rescue all sixteen sailors from the *Hibernia*.

The *W.C. Hite*, a ship bound for Jeffersonville, was turned around in midstream by the tornado. The *Hite* made it to its destination anyway, the only damage having been done to the nerves of its passengers.

After visiting Louisville's waterfront, the killer cyclone crossed the broad Ohio and moved into Jeffersonville, Indiana. It performed prodigious property damage in that city but barely touched New Albany. The death toll in both places was zero. Perhaps the Hoosiers saw it coming and

Tenth and Main. *Wilburn Stereographs; 99.36.042; Special Collections, University of Louisville.*

had time to take shelter. After sampling the southern tip of Indiana, the tornado turned around, crossed the river again and came back to Louisville, where it demolished the city's waterworks, an improbably elegant, classical-looking building complete with Grecian columns. The tornado journeyed across the countryside to Carroll County, where at last it dissipated, gone and not in the least lamented.

There is a silver lining behind every cloud—even funnel clouds—and in some respects the Louisville disaster, awful as it was, could have been much worse. Although many boats on the waterfront had been yanked loose from their moorings, surprisingly little damage was done to steamboats and tugboats. Some coal boats sank, but not a single life was lost on the river. Due to broken gaslights and open fireplaces, an estimated half-dozen separate fires soon were raging throughout the stricken area. Luckily, some were extinguished when collapsing debris cut off their oxygen supply. Had the tornado struck farther west, it would have destroyed factories and done immeasurable harm to the city's economy. Despite the storm's violence and the heavy rain that preceded it, the creaky dam at the Point did not burst, as many had worried. If it had, Louisville would have faced a flood as well as a tornado and several fires. The storm's timing was fortunate: it had struck at night rather than in the daytime when schools would have been full of children, offices full of workers and streets full of shoppers. And at least the tornado had missed the city's theatre district. Had it hit one or more of the packed theatres, scores of additional lives might have been lost. As it turned out, Louisville's theatre patrons had no idea the storm had struck until they left for home—some discovering that they no longer had a home to go to.

On the larger scale, even better news came after Sergeant Dunn, head of the New York Signal Corps office—who called the Louisville tornado "the greatest calamity in the history of the country"—predicted that a tidal wave would issue from the Mississippi River and destroy everything in its path. The oddly slow-moving flood would reach Cairo, Illinois, about April 1 and would destroy New Orleans in three weeks. The good news was that Dunn was mistaken.

PART III

After

At this writing no definite statement can be made of the loss of life, but it is large. It is impossible that so wide a sweep of territory covered with ruined homes, with wrecked halls and buildings of every character does not contain many dead, which only the light of the sun can reveal. Enough is known to show that Louisville has been visited by a most appalling calamity, and that her citizens who have escaped must respond readily, today, to every call for relief. It need not be said this city will, as in the past, care for its own.

—editorial, Courier-Journal, *March 28, 1890*

It was all over in five minutes. The temperature, which had risen to a relatively balmy sixty-eight degrees just before the tornado, dropped to thirty-nine degrees after it passed. There was neither rain nor hail immediately afterward; instead, by a sarcastic act of nature, the clouds parted and a brilliant moon illuminated the scenes of destruction below—a moon that seemed blood red due to the strange haze in the atmosphere, as Hazel Miller remembered seventy years later. Rescue efforts began right away, centering at first on the devastated Falls City Hall. H.C. Aylsworth witnessed the building's collapse as he stood in a doorway on Market Street. Aylsworth and L. Vance, a butcher, undertook the task of crawling into a small tunnel formed by the chance arrangement of fallen debris, located where the stairway once was, with illumination provided only by a lantern. (The deed was rendered even more perilous by escaping gas.) They crawled into what Aylsworth called an "apartment" formed by interlocking rafters that supported pieces of the building. He later described a scene from a living nightmare:

> *I arose to my feet and, holding the lantern above my head, gazed around. The scene that met my eyes will never be forgotten to my dying day. Out from the crevices between the heavy timbers protruded the hands and feet of human beings. But the most appalling of all were the gleaming eyes, almost ready to burst from their sockets, which we saw watching us from several portions of the room.*

Despite their own feelings of terror, Aylsworth and Vance managed to carry out some of the dead and several injured people, including a twelve-year-old girl named Eva Witherspoon. Policemen and civilians—including women—quickly arrived after Aylsworth and Vance and immediately began the arduous task of removing debris and rescuing the wounded or retrieving the dead, unmindful of the risks posed by teetering wreckage, fire and gas escaping from pipes. It took an hour of digging before they uncovered the first victim, Mrs. Sarah Kelly, who had only a broken arm and some bruises. She told her rescuers an ugly story about the wild panic that occurred in the hall when its occupants comprehended that a tornado was upon them: there was a rush for the entrance, during which women were knocked to the floor and trampled. The doorway was congested with too many people trying to squeeze through, so Mrs. Kelly and several friends decided to stay put and trust in fate. The last thing she remembered was seeing the floor collapse and the ceiling fall. Rescuers found none of the people who had taken shelter near her.

When the rescuers pulled a live little girl out of the wreckage, cheers resounded for blocks.

As the workmen excavated, they found most of the bodies in the hallways and on the stairs at the rear of the building. The victims had tried to flee but were unable to open the locked doors when the structure collapsed on them. At the front of the building, excavators found ten women "locked in each other's arms," nine of whom were dead. The press reported a painful incident: "Mr. James Hassan, whose wife had been at the lodge meeting, was foremost in the work, and the first person he drew out of the ruined building was his wife, who died in his arms. He laid her by the side of the others who were dead, and continued to work for the living." Tragically, a young couple was found holding each other

Falls City Hall. *Wilburn Stereographs; 99.36.011; Special Collections, University of Louisville.*

in death, "her arms clasped around his neck while he held her about the waist." Their heads were mangled and "their limbs crushed into a shapeless mass." Thirty more bodies were found, all without injuries; it was thought that these victims had died of suffocation during the panic or while buried alive in the debris. They may have died from inhaling fumes emitted by broken gas pipes. It is a good idea to hide in a closet when a tornado approaches, but that did not save three little girls found dead in what had been a third-floor closet. The *Courier-Journal* noted: "Their bodies, when found, were moist as if death had come to them as their rescuers approached."

Some of the dead were kept at one part of the destroyed building until they could be taken to the morgue; some bodies were taken to the closest undertaking establishment, Dougherty and Keenan's, located a block away; and some bodies were temporarily stored in intact houses across the street, no doubt to the distress of the homeowners. F.W. Link's barbershop was commandeered for use as a temporary morgue. The injured were treated at nearby houses and offices; some were carried into saloons, where counters and pool tables were utilized as hospital beds.

Parents whose children had been attending the dancing class came to the scene, but police kept them away. Louis Simm Jr. escaped the tornado's wrath, but he was so frightened during the event that later he had no idea how. He went to the wreckage of the Falls City Hall to find his wife and four daughters; when the area where the dancing school had been was unearthed at 11:30 p.m., the badly injured Mrs. Simm was the first person unearthed. Within fifteen minutes, three of Simm's unconscious daughters had been restored to him. However, before the night was over, death would claim two of Simm's children—Geneva, age four, and Louis, age six—as well as his clerk, George Foster. To cap the tragedy, Simm later found that his combination house and furniture store, located next to the hall, had burned down.

The children of Annie Niles were rendered orphans by the tornado; worse, their only guardian, their uncle John Renouf, also died of injuries received at the hall.

George Schmitt ran a saloon on Market Street, opposite Falls City Hall, and was president of the Falls City Market. Ironically, his saloon was barely scratched by the tornado. Had he stayed there instead of crossing the street to visit the hall, he would have survived.

At midnight, just after a man named John Hepden was rescued, the disaster became even worse: when a large piece of debris was lifted, a draft fanned a small fire. The wreckage became ablaze. Aylsworth and Vance, still undergoing their rescue attempts, had to abandon some victims. Said Aylsworth:

> *It was getting so hot that we could scarcely reach the last man we went after. Right by his side was another man pinned down by some timbers. When we started away, leaving him there as I knew to die, I could not resist the impulse to grasp his hand and tell him goodbye. "Goodbye," he said, hopefully, "Come back quick after me." Poor fellow, he did not know that the fire had cut us off, and that we had made our last trip.*

The moans of those still trapped became screams as they faced death not by crushing nor by suffocation but by burning. The sight so horrified and disheartened many bystanders that they fled the scene rather than witness any more. Firefighters extinguished the flames, but at the cost of another precious hour.

Several hundred laborers continued digging at Falls City Hall. Night crews had their work illuminated by newfangled electric lights. Body after body was pulled from the wreckage. It was feared at first that 150 people had been killed there; by April 5, the total was determined to be closer to 44. (The toll was likely closer to 50; see appendix.) The first floor of the hall consisted of shops, all of which were closed when the tornado struck. Had they been open and full of customers at the fatal moment, the death toll certainly would have been much higher.

Of the estimated 65 men, women and children who had been in Miss App's dancing studio, only 15 survived. Of the 7 members of the Roman Knights fraternity, only Theodore Engelmeier was killed. (Engelmeier was found holding the funeral notice of a friend who had died a couple of weeks before.) Seventeen members of the Humboldt Lodge of the Odd Fellows met on the third floor; the ones who didn't die were badly injured. An estimated 150 people were on the third floor attending the meeting of the Jewel Lodge of the Knights and Ladies of Honor; it was thought that only a dozen had escaped death, but fortunately this proved unfounded: most had left the building before the tornado struck. Twenty Knights and Ladies were killed at Falls City Hall, and 35 were wounded.

There were stories of hairbreadth escapes. Amazingly, all officers of the Jewel Lodge were found alive. One, George Capito, described what a reporter called "a thrilling experience, and one that he has no desire to repeat." Capito remembered that the building had rocked twice and then a dormer window exploded. A mass exodus for the anteroom ensued, and just as the party reached the door, the floor collapsed. Fortunately for Capito, the door frame fell with him and landed in such a way as to protect him from falling debris. He was able to tunnel his way into an adjoining house, where he kicked open the doors and stepped out onto the street, relatively uninjured and breathing in the bracing night air. He returned to the scene of the disaster to help put out a fire.

Annie App, who taught dancing classes in the doomed building, was buried in the wreckage along with most of her students. She was rescued but suffered from crushed hips and legs. As she recuperated at her parents' house, she told a reporter a horrifying tale. Just before the storm hit, she had been demonstrating the waltz with a young man named Moses Lazarus. Her students had begun following her lead when the large double doors on the room's east side blew open repeatedly despite the attempts of several men to keep them closed.

Miss App instructed her assistant, Katie Frazier, to keep playing the piano in order to prevent a panic. At last, the door opened with so much force that it hurled the men holding it "like so much straw," as Miss App phrased it. The windows shattered and rain poured in, but the lights remained unextinguished. Despite the teacher's efforts, the students ran about the room in wild fright. The building rocked; the floor moved up and down; Miss App headed for the stairway. On the way, she saw a student, William Heeb, also running to the exit "with a woman clinging to him." The floor caved in, and when Miss App woke up, she was underneath a door with three cartloads of the former Falls City Hall on top of it. She cried out, "Please help me, save me." A man's voice responded, "I can't help you for I am covered with bricks." Three hours later, rescuers pulled Miss App out. She never discovered whether her companion in the darkness lived or died.

J.T. "Tom" Funk—a member of the Jewel Lodge who had for months been trying to convince the other members to hold their meetings in Euclid Hall on the grounds that the stairs at Falls City Hall were too steep—had been standing by the lodge's altar when a load of bricks, mortar and hail crashed through an east window. Funk corroborated Capito's statement that the terrified crowd had run for the lodge anteroom. From his vantage point, Funk could see that the room was certain to be buried if the building fell, and he forcibly pulled everyone he could reach out of it. The east wall collapsed; a half minute later, Funk estimated, the west wall crumbled. Amid the sound of snapping timbers, breaking bones and the cries of the injured and dying, the floor gave way, and Funk was thrown two floors down. He landed on his feet, but he was pinned by debris and bodies, lost in total blackness and discomfited by the shrill whistle of the tornado's winds over his head. The east side of the third floor fell, bringing at least fifty people with it. Seconds later, they were crushed by the collapsing back wall, west wall and roof.

As Funk stood partially buried, he could hear the creaking of nearby timbers, the cries of the buried and the departing tornado destroying other buildings as it made its way to the riverfront. He found the whole thing a trying experience. He managed to painfully extricate himself—fearing all the while that he would be flattened by debris if the timbers broke—and made his way to the street. Blood-soaked, with a mouthful of mortar and splinters and seeking assistance, he crawled on all fours over bricks, cornices and other fragments of buildings. He collapsed several times from exhaustion in the cold, deep mud. When at last he reached a dry goods store across the street, he feebly knocked on the door, only to hear a woman inside say: "Shut that door! That man's drunk!"

Another survivor, saloonkeeper Henry Felthoelton, was buried in the wreckage. He had been on the second floor, directly beneath the Knights and Ladies of Honor lodge room, when the upper floor collapsed. Felthoelton spent two and a half hours wedged between two pieces of timber, listening to the moans of the dying, "wild shrieks from the uninjured" and excited voices from outside. He heard a woman praying above him:

> *I cannot remember the words, but her prayer was for the deliverance of all but herself. Just as this one voice was ascending like hope from the grave, someone from on top of the wreck cried that the mass was on fire. I shall never forget my own feelings, or the maddening screams of the terror-stricken women above me. I felt that death was approaching me in a way I had not expected.*

Felthoelton believed that some of the women at Falls City Hall died of fright upon hearing the unthinking person's cry that the wreckage was on fire. According to press reports, the saloonkeeper had a head full of jet black hair before being entombed by the tornado; when rescued, his hair allegedly was streaked with gray and white.

An unrecognizable corpse was determined to be Tom Puff after it was washed. "No man in the West End had more friends than Puff, and he was universally liked," read a news report. A German band attached to the Louisville Legion militia, consisting of fifteen members, was thought to have perished in the collapsing building. Nineteen-year-old William Heeb was found dead, "very little disfigured, and his face wore a peaceful expression." He wore upon his vest a gold badge he had won years before in a roller-skating contest. When the body of George Foster was found, it was sent to undertaker Christ Miller's establishment—but Miller himself was dead, lying in the center of the hall's remains. The mortician was not disfigured, and it was theorized that he had survived for hours under the rubble until he suffocated.

When rescuers found a body, it would be washed and placed in temporary storage—often, a store or saloon across the street—until the identifiable ones could be taken by relatives to a funeral parlor. A reporter related that virtually all corpses "had a look of horror upon their faces, showing plainly that they must have feared the consequences when the tornado first struck the fated hall."

Falls City Hall. *Wilburn Stereographs; 99.36.019; Special Collections, University of Louisville.*

On March 29, the last body was removed from the ruins of the Falls City Hall: Annie App's final dancing partner, Moses Lazarus. His body was found separated from the others; judging from its location, it was surmised that he had been trying to escape through a locked rear door when death overtook him. "The face was bruised and swollen from the falling bricks and was of a purple color," observed a reporter. "The neck must have been broken when the building fell, and death is supposed to have ensued immediately." But the announcement that the last victim had been extracted did not convince a madman who arrived at the site the next day. He escaped the attention of the militia guarding the area and, convinced that his brother's remains were undiscovered, set to work digging in the debris with his bare hands. A crowd gathered; the militiamen attempted unsuccessfully to encourage him to move on, telling him that if a body was in the wreckage, they would find it. The stranger addressed the crowd in very elegant and poetic language, considering that he was a lunatic: "Tonight, when you demons are reveling in the delights of the world, I will be here covered with the sad snow hunting for my lost brother. If you all had hearts you would not try to make me move. You would take off your coats and set to work rescuing the dead." Eventually, he found part of a burned hat and, kissing this relic, walked away.

On March 31, Mayor Jacob dismissed the militia that had been guarding Falls City Hall. The search for bodies at that site was officially over. All that remained was for the area to be cleaned up and for the families of victims to assuage their grief as best they could.

Though Falls City Hall was the worst deathtrap in Louisville and thus got the most attention in the press, it was not the only scene of desolation. When the extent of the tornado's devastation became known on the night of the disaster, attempts to retrieve the dead and rescue the living were made in other parts of the city. Frank Smith, a pressman, entered the ruins of R.H. Carother's printing firm on the corner of Eighth and Main; in the basement, he found a beautiful, bejeweled woman (probably Ada Helm) dead under some timbers. He took two bracelets and some other jewelry—for purposes not mentioned in news reports—and soon was overcome by gas fumes. He was rescued by two men, who turned the jewelry over to the police.

When a tornado devastates an area today, witnesses often state that it looks like a nuclear bomb exploded there. But in 1890, long before such powerful weapons were invented, people had nothing in their experience to which they could compare the storm's destruction. With the dawn, citizens saw roofs lying in the streets, columns of debris, mountains of bricks, oceans of broken glass and desolate chimneys standing where once stood two- and three-story Victorian mansions. In some places, only single walls stood; in other places, nothing. Businesses had top floors missing or the front shaved off. Here and there, smoke curled upward from the midst of a pile of debris. Trees ranging from saplings to enormous old sentinels were toppled, their roots standing higher than a man's head. Other trees had withstood the storm but were festooned with wires and strips of tin roofs. Telegraph poles were leaning or down, entangled in one another's wires. Store items and personal possessions were strewn everywhere. Dead horses spotted the ruined landscape, their legs and heads twisted at unnatural angles and with boards sticking out of their bodies. And there were the many dead, lying under sheets or exposed to view, their horrendous injuries guaranteed to give a lifetime's worth of nightmares to everyone who saw them.

Louisville officials discovered that the city was cut off from the rest of the world: all of the telegraph and telephone lines had been destroyed. Any help that Louisville was going to get in those first critical hours was going to have to come from within. Survivors were unable to wire friends and family outside the city and inform them that they had lived. News of the tornado spread beyond Louisville, thanks to Mr. Arnold of the Western Union office, who rode a boat to Jeffersonville, Indiana, and from there wired the information to Indianapolis.

Though it may defy belief in our high-tech age when television broadcasts news as quickly as possible and the Internet provides us with instant information about every major and minor disaster, the majority of Louisvillians did not live in the disaster area and had no idea that a killer tornado had hit their city. They found out about it only when they opened their morning newspapers. Fifty years after the event, former resident John Doyle remembered his surprise when his brother-in-law burst through the door and said, "Are you aware that nearly all of Louisville has been blown to pieces tonight by a cyclone?"

Once the word got out, the inevitable sightseers congested the sidewalks to gawk at the scenes of nature's destruction—also, as a sour commentary on human nature, opportunistic ghouls, thieves and looters prowled the streets looking for an opportunity to rob the living or the dead. Someone stole a diamond pin from a dead woman who lay on the floor of Buckley's Saloon, but his conscience must have bothered him because he later returned it. Bridget Horan had had $300 on her person when she was killed at Falls City Hall; it disappeared during excavation work and was likely taken by a workman, since the militia kept morbidly curious citizens away from the wreckage. An undertaker's assistant named Boyd was arrested on a charge of stealing money from the corpse of Charles Jenks. Entire gangs of would-be thieves arrived by boat to loot the remains of the Union Depot, which held passengers' luggage and $100,000 worth of railway tickets. The police arrived at the scene first and promised to shoot anyone who tried it, whereupon the boats turned around and the thieves slunk back to whatever hole they had crawled out of. On the morning of March 28, the governor ordered 250 militiamen

Tornado damage; location unknown. *Wilburn Stereographs; 99.36.052; Special Collections, University of Louisville.*

from the Louisville Legion into service to protect property from looters and aid the overworked police.

An ominous discovery was made the morning after the cyclone: it had destroyed the standpipe at the city waterworks. Two engineers, Captain Weist and C.D. Merrit, had been on night duty on March 27. Both survived despite the tornado's best efforts to kill them. Merrit recalled that the first sign of trouble was a strong wind, followed by shattering windows. The roar of the winds turned into a shrill whistle, and the roof collapsed on Weist and Merrit. The engines continued turning faster and faster; then, they abruptly stopped. When the howling ceased, the engineers looked outside and found that the building was surrounded by water. Although the pumping station's standpipe was 160 feet high, made of brick and iron and surrounded by a wooden casing, the tornado had wrenched off a large section and threw it 50 feet. Consequently, Louisville had only a six-day supply of fresh water for drinking or first aid. The store of water had been drained by the previous night's firefighting efforts.

Union Depot. *Wilburn Stereographs; 99.36.018; Special Collections, University of Louisville.*

Louisvillians consumed an estimated twelve million gallons of water per day; this had to be reduced to three million until further notice. Charles R. Long, president of the water company, requested that citizens use water only for purposes of drinking, cooking and putting out fires.

Much monetary loss to the city, to say nothing of incalculable personal inconvenience, resulted from the loss of the state-of-the-art Union Depot. Though loss of life there was minimal, the sight of the wrecked depot seemed to dispirit onlookers more than anything except the ruins of Falls City Hall. Here, after all, was one place where virtually everyone in the city had been at some time, whether to go on trips or pick up friends and relatives. On March 27, it had been the pride of the city; on March 28, it was a heap of destroyed train cars and debris. It had been one of the Falls City's hubs of commerce. The passengers, porters, conductors, engineers and ticket agents were gone, replaced by a single man with a rifle to intimidate looters. It was several days before trains could be received and sent on their way as usual.

It was time for the citizens of Louisville to roll up their sleeves and get to work. This they did with haste and attention to detail. The city council immediately appropriated $20,000 for the relief of storm victims; private parties contributed the same amount. In modern currency, this $40,000 would be equivalent to almost $1 million. The city's Board of Trade, acting in conjunction with Mayor Charles D. Jacob, formed the General Relief Committee of the Board of Trade. Two subcommittees were founded. The Executive Committee oversaw everything and disbursed money from a common fund; the Committee of Visitation and Inspection visited every house in the stricken district, taking down the names of survivors and inquiring as to their immediate necessities. These civic-minded businessmen made sure that sufferers got the materials they needed and later provided them with funds for house repairs. (The reader will observe that by personally checking out each case, these capitalists of the often-maligned private sector screened out fakers who tried to get charity under false pretenses and made sure that every dollar went where it could do the most good. This is in contrast to the modern plan, in which government bureaucracies throw truckloads of taxpayers' cash around after a disaster and hope for the best.)

Further aid came from the Commercial Club, which, among other things, helped the Louisville Legion militia police the streets. The *Courier-Journal*'s columns were filled with lists of individuals and businesses that contributed funds. The Kentucky Wagon Manufacturing Company made arrangements with an old-fashioned-sounding musical group called the Old Hickory Quintet to put on a benefit show. The Louisville and Nashville Railroad donated $10,000; the *Courier-Journal*, $250; and the *Louisville Times*, $100. Frank Harris of the Northern Lake Ice Company offered to let the city use his ice wagons for any purpose. The Ministerial Association and, it appears, every church in town collected money to aid sufferers. Just to name one example out of a great many, the Ladies' Aid Society of East Baptist Church held a benefit luncheon, with profits going straight to charity. Virtually every theatre in Louisville held special matinees and concerts, the proceeds from which went to relieve local suffering. The Flower Mission, a charitable group, set to work offering relief and comfort. A benefit concert was held at the Masonic Temple under the direction of Colonel Will Hays, Louisville's noted songwriter. (Again, it is worth noting that churches, businessmen, fraternal organizations, relief committees formed by private citizens and charities—not the government—provided the most help for the poor and needy, and they did it very successfully and without waste.)

The actor Richard Mansfield, famous for his performances in *Richard III* and *Dr. Jekyll and Mr. Hyde*, appeared at Macauley's Theatre the week after the tornado and pledged to donate his entire receipts to the homeless. The members of the Odd Fellows, the Knights and Ladies of Honor and the Roman Knights helped the families of their stricken members. The governors of Ohio and Indiana, the mayors of New York and Boston, the Cincinnati Chamber of Commerce and officers representing the Masonic Lodges of Ohio volunteered to send money. Mayor Jacob told them that while he would not appeal for help outside of Louisville, he would gladly accept any voluntary contributions. Nevertheless, he diplomatically turned down most outside offers of help, saying that Louisville would accept charity only if and when its own resources were exhausted. Touchingly, the Relief Fund in Louisville received $500 from the residents of Johnstown, Pennsylvania, who had themselves been victims the previous year of one of the most disastrous floods in American history. Louisville's rich and poor alike opened their homes to victims until they found permanent lodgings. At Parkland, Clem Kremer allowed thirty refugees of the storm to live in his house until their own homes could be repaired or they could find someplace else to live, by which we deduce that Mr. Kremer must have had a large house.

On March 28, the Kentucky legislature proposed appropriating $25,000 to help tornado victims in Louisville and across the state; on April 1, this amount was increased to $30,000 (modern equivalent: $705,000). The appropriation passed without debate on April 2. As of that date, funds sent to the Board of Trade's General Relief Committee had amounted to $73,785; donations sent to Mayor Jacob, including the money raised by the city appropriation, amounted to about $50,000. (Altogether, the modern equivalent of this sum would be almost $3 million.) In striking contrast to the modern welfare state, some victims proudly refused help, as was pointed out in a March 30 *Courier-Journal* article entitled "Help," which detailed the relief measures being enacted in the city, state and outside the state. Mayor Jacob said, "I saw much distress and suffering, but the people are brave and hopeful and few are asking help, but many are refusing to accept it when offered to them when they can possibly get on without it."

Ninth and Main, looking west. *Wilburn Stereographs; 99.36.036; Special Collections, University of Louisville.*

As incredible as it may seem, Louisville cleaned up its wreckage, tended to its injured and rebuilt its economy with *no assistance whatsoever from the federal government*. This was a matter of no small civic pride. A couple of days after the disaster, the *Courier-Journal* boasted in an editorial entitled "Relief Measures," "The people of Louisville are both able and willing to furnish all the means that the Relief Commission requires. No appeal will be made for assistance abroad. Our people hold it both a matter of pride and privilege to relieve the suffering of our own citizens." Similarly, an editorial published on March 30 stated, "The citizens of Louisville appreciate fully the offers of assistance coming from all sections of the country…[U]ntil the citizens of Louisville have themselves done all that is in their power to do it is not just to our friends that we should accept anything but kind words." Similar

Market Street. *Wilburn Stereographs; 99.36.021; Special Collections, University of Louisville.*

expressions of determined independence were expressed in editorials entitled "No Outside Aid Needed" (March 31), "The Work of Relief" (April 1)—which referred to Louisville's vow to help its own citizens to its fullest ability before appealing to outside aid, "a noble vindication of the 'Kentucky Idea' of self-government founded on self-reliance"—and "The City's Boast" (April 3).

The city was even reluctant to accept aid from the State of Kentucky, as expressed in an editorial called "State Aid": "Louisville recognizes the fact that the duty of relieving the suffering among her own citizens rests first on herself, and it is a duty which she would not willingly transfer even to our own good State of Kentucky." The city's heroic demonstration of independence was not lost on the press in other states: the *New York Mail and Express* praised Louisville's refusal to "accept, if not to invite, outside

Tenth and Main, looking east. *Wilburn Stereographs; 99.36.037; Special Collections, University of Louisville.*

aid...Even the suggestions of state assistance made in the Kentucky Legislature were not encouraged because the people of Louisville feel that they are equal to the emergency." The *Memphis Appeal* saw both the nation's generosity and Louisville's reluctance to accept it as illustrations of a healthy spirit: "This goes to show how closely the people of every section are allied, notwithstanding the immense intervening distances. The lavishness of the display of this form of charity is one of the proofs of the immense wealth of the country." Similar sentiments were expressed by the *Columbus Post*, *Albany Express*, *Columbus Journal*, *Providence Journal* and *Chicago Globe*.

Louisville did such a good job of "taking care of her own" that when Red Cross founder Clara Barton and two assistants arrived on March 30, they saw that their assistance was not necessary and left.

The tornado damaged or destroyed countless houses and places of business on the smaller cross streets that connected with Louisville's main thoroughfares. There were no bulldozers and dump trucks in 1890, so every scrap of the heavy debris had to be cleared with the oldest tool known to history: the human hand. The city paid 120 laborers; half worked all day and half worked all night. The Relief Committee paid for additional workers. They certainly had their work cut out for them; in some places on Market Street, the storm left thirty-foot piles of rubble. On Jefferson Street, passersby saw signs on houses offering laborers then-extravagant wages of $3, $4 or $5 for a day's work (equivalent to up to $117 in modern currency). Within three days, the streets were cleared enough to admit throngs of reporters from other cities—and sightseers. The police and militia had kept ghouls and the merely curious away from the ruins of Falls City Hall, but after the discovery of the final corpse, they received orders that tourists would be allowed to view the site as long as they were orderly and the line kept moving. On March 30, an estimated 100,000 people, mostly from Louisville and southern Indiana—but some from distant towns in Kentucky, as well as St. Louis, Cincinnati, Chicago and Indianapolis—got in line and filed by the place where scores of their fellow humans had perished miserably at the hands of nature. "There were rich and poor, black and white, young and old, of all classes and nationalities," wrote a reporter, "and yet all had a word of sympathy for the homeless and a word of consolation for the bereaved." Some brought gifts for survivors. The tourists were notably silent, thoughtful and well behaved. The pile of scorched fragments formerly known as the Virgil Wright building also was a popular attraction, as were the ruined tobacco district and the streets lined with destroyed houses.

The technology of 1890 was not advanced enough to allow reproductions of photographs in newspapers, so in addition to reporters and rubberneckers, Louisville saw an influx of newspaper artists from around the nation who came to sketch the destruction. Comparing the artists' drawings to photos of the ruins reveals that their renderings were quite accurate. Only recently had George Eastman invented the Kodak camera, making amateur photography a phenomenon. As a result, the streets of Louisville were choked not only with professional photographers (notably Edward Klauber), who made pictures to sell as souvenirs, but also tourists snapping their own shots. Photographs showing the nearly inconceivable violence wrought by the cyclone exist in university archives and historical collections. No doubt many more are preserved in old

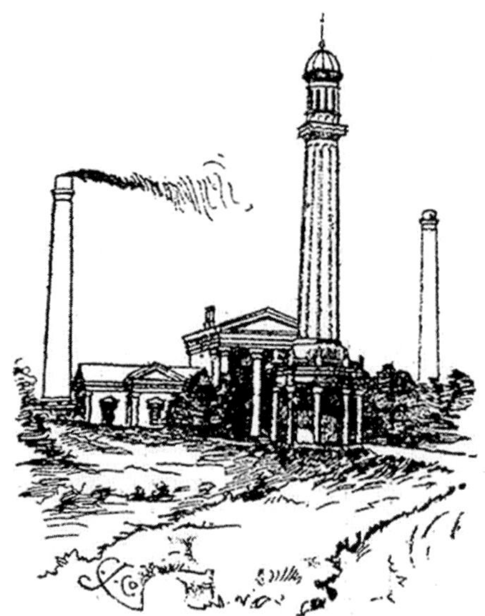

The waterworks before the tornado. *Louisville Courier-Journal*, April 7, 1890. *Courtesy of the* Courier-Journal.

The waterworks after. *Louisville Courier-Journal*, April 11, 1890. *Courtesy of the* Courier-Journal.

family albums and in a multitude of trunks in a multitude of attics. Such photos allow modern scientists to estimate the storm's destructive force. According to Thomas Grazulis, author of *Significant Tornados*, the Great Louisville Tornado would have measured an F4 on the Fujita Scale, by which climatologists estimate a tornado's power based on the damage it inflicts on trees and structures. (The highest reading on the scale is F5.)

One improvement came when Louisville got back its water supply. It had seemed as though the city would face a "water famine" for an extended length of time. Despite repeated entreaties to ration water, Louisvillians had not obeyed, and the city faced a crisis that affected everyone, not just the blocks hit by the tornado. Repairmen toiled at the damaged waterworks around the clock. Luckily for the city, while the standpipe had been destroyed, the engines used to pump water were unharmed. A temporary, and entirely experimental, standpipe was constructed. No one was sure if it would work. "Suspense," said an eye-catching *Courier-Journal* headline, which continued in a sub-headline: "The Improvised Stand-Pipe Yet to Be Tested. In Case It Works, the Reservoir Will Be Filled. If It Fails the City Will Experience a Water Famine." On April 2, the apparatus was turned on, and to the immense relief of everyone, it worked perfectly. By the next day, river water was being pumped into the reservoir at the accustomed rate.

Relief also came when the city's telegraph and telephone lines were partially repaired early on March 28; by March 30, Louisville was again able to contact other places. (On March 31, the Western Union wire services were completely restored.) After the tornado struck, it was rumored that only three houses were left standing in Parkland, a suburb southwest of the city, but no one could confirm it. When the telegraph system was fixed, it was found that while Parkland had been struck, destruction there was not as bad as was previously thought. Thousands of dollars in damage had been wrought and thirteen houses were destroyed—J.G. Brown's house was turned upside-down—but no lives had been lost. A *Courier-Journal* editorial appearing on March 29 mentioned the city's isolation before the lines were replaced: "The want of telegraphic communication with the outer world prevents us at this writing from forming an intelligent opinion as to the extent of the loss in other sections…[T]he worst may not be known for several days."

When contact with the world beyond Louisville was restored, citizens discovered that they were not alone in their misery: other places in Kentucky had also been hit on March 27, including the counties of Laurel, Graves, Henry, Shelby, Caldwell, Barren and Trigg. Fifty persons were killed or seriously injured in Webster County. A tornado left a trail of destruction thirty miles long and a quarter-mile wide in Crittenden County. Grand Rivers, a new manufacturing town in Livingston County, was virtually wiped out; two were killed there and seven died altogether in the county. William Hayden, a railroad bridge watchman at Kuttawa, Lyon County, heard the sound of a gigantic tornado sucking up trees as it approached. He survived by running to the mainland, throwing himself flat on the ground and wrapping his arms around an iron rail. Near Hopkinsville, Christian County, a tornado threw a tree across railroad tracks, wrecking a train and killing the engineer, the fireman and the brakeman. From Blackford, Union County, came the remarkable tale of W.J. Dulaney, a farmer whose house was demolished. Dulaney's small daughter Florence was killed and his wife injured, yet despite his personal loss, he remembered that a train headed for Princeton was due to run by. Dulaney built a signal fire to warn the locomotive engineer that trees were down across the track, saving the lives of up to one hundred passengers.

In all, nearly sixty people were killed by tornados in western Kentucky on March 27, not including the death toll in Louisville. Nine were killed in Livingston County; eight in Webster; four in Ohio; four in Daviess; eight in Breckinridge; one in Grayson; two in Lyon; six in Christian; and seventeen in Allen. Killer tornados also struck several towns in Tennessee.

The tornado had delivered a blow to Louisville, but it was hardly a knockout. The *Courier-Journal*'s business report datelined March 28 noted that while commerce had been stalled for a day, there was a "confident and hopeful feeling on Main Street. The work of cleaning away the ruins had already begun, and the task of rebuilding will not long be delayed. Business has received only a momentary check, and its full tide will soon flow in the old channels." Elsewhere on the same page, the newspaper remarked with optimism: "[T]he loss is not so great as it at first appeared. There is already a reaction and returning energies. In counting over losses we should count fairly, face the future fearlessly, and in a month's time, as far as mere material effect is concerned, the tornado will be a tale that is told." In an April 4 editorial, the general feeling of encouragement was expressed by a businessman whom the *Courier-Journal* described as "a self-made and comparatively young man, the heaviest financial sufferer by the storm," who declared: "If God spares me life and strength I will earn it all back again."

In fact, some merchants increased business *because* of the tornado, including telegraph services such as Western Union, streetcars and, of course, carpenters and suppliers of building materials. Hotels profitably housed out-of-towners who came to Louisville to see the damage. Hundreds of unemployed men found temporary work as night watchmen or removers of debris. On March 30, the newspaper said in an editorial:

Tenth and Main, looking west. *Wilburn Stereographs; 99.36.038; Special Collections, University of Louisville.*

> *This is not discouraging; it is a loss the city can stand without any serious effect on business…The outlook is not gloomy, it is full of inspiration. We have been subject to a great calamity; we have suffered heavily; but we have shown our faith in ourselves; we have manifested a spirit of self-reliance; a devotion to the common welfare, and a power of organization that constitute the best possible assurance which could possibly offer future commercial success.*

The stricken district was so well cleaned up by March 31—and the police and militia had so efficiently prevented looting and lawlessness, and business had recovered so quickly—that Mayor Jacob could say, with understandable pride, that "as far as the public is concerned, order has never been better, and outside of the narrow limits of the district swept by the storm, no one would know that he was in a city that had been scourged by a fierce and most devastating tornado."

In the days following the tornado, readers of the *Courier-Journal* saw a sure sign that the city was recovering: merchants placed advertisements reassuring customers that their goods were untouched and ready for sale. For example, a March 31 ad for Tapp, Leathers, and Co. stated that although its building had been hit, the company had regained most of its stock and had set up business in temporary quarters. In the same issue, the Wheeler Carriage company offered to sell "cyclone bargains"; that is, carriages "only slightly defaced by dust and dirt from the debris, and...as durable and substantial as ever." Snead and Bibb, blacksmiths, advertised that they had "a large force of men ready for repair work." Some businesses offered items at greatly reduced prices for tornado victims. A March 29 ad for Levy's clothing store urged: "The unfortunate ones are earnestly invited to call and unhesitatingly ask for what they need; but we beg of others not to attempt to take advantage of this offer. We want to help the NEEDY, not those who are able to help themselves." (Some businesses even capitalized on the tornado. A year and a half later, on September 20, 1891, Levy's ran an ad featuring a drawing of a tornado throwing men's suits around and promising an "Autumn Cyclone" of bargains.)

Carpenters rebuilt warehouses in the tobacco district so quickly that it reminded some observers of the construction of a prairie town. Fortunately, the tobacco warehouses were not as badly damaged as had been supposed at first, though they certainly were damaged enough. By March 30, business in the path of the tornado was more or less back to normal. Merchants whose stores had been destroyed simply arranged to sell their goods in other parts of the city. "They are all full of hope," editorialized the *Courier-Journal*, "and there is scarcely one among them who will not triumph over misfortune." On April 1, it was observed that merchants were as busy as ever and "expected no further interruptions to business." On April 4, the *Courier-Journal* could state in an editorial: "Business was never better than it has been here this week. Main Street from one end to the other has been crowded, and merchants are making heavy shipments of goods." The resilience of the human spirit was well illustrated by the merchants of Louisville, who refused to surrender to the calamity wrought upon them, who cleaned up and got back to work as soon as possible and who in many cases triumphed with better buildings and more business than they had before the storm.

Private residences, too, were repaired if they were damaged slightly—or, if they were total losses, razed and rebuilt—at amazing speed. Hammers clanked away constantly from dawn to dusk as dozens of tinners fixed hundreds of roofs. Even a heavy snowstorm and the Sabbath stopped neither the carpenters nor the sightseers. The brick makers and bricklayers who had gone on strike a few days before were back at work; they indignantly denied rumors that they were charging grossly inflated rates for their work. They even resolved to give the proceeds of their May Day demonstration to tornado victims.

Many persons whose buildings had been destroyed by fire found, to their disappointment, that their policies did not cover their losses on the grounds that the tornado demolished the buildings *before* they caught fire. A.G. Langham, a local insurance agent, explained that a building hit by a tornado immediately ceased to be a building. He also noted that one direct result of the cyclone had been a sudden, understandable interest in tornado insurance—a commodity that, the reader will recall, had not overly concerned Louisvillians in years past. One Louisville firm, the German Mutual Fire Insurance Company, announced on March 31 that policyholders whose buildings were burned after being hit by the tornado would receive payment in full. This was a good public relations move. In the future, the company was not shy about reminding people of the calamity that had once struck their city.

While one might have expected insurance firms to be bankrupted by the tornado, it was estimated that the life and accident insurance companies of Louisville had to pay out only between $100,000 and $125,000 (modern equivalent: between $2,350,000 and $3,000,000). One of the heaviest financial burdens was met not by a major insurance company but by the Knights and Ladies of Honor. Like most fraternal orders, the group offered an insurance plan to its members; the heirs of those killed by the twister were entitled to $2,000 (modern equivalent: nearly $50,000). On March 29, the surviving members met to get to the grim business of determining how many of their number had died at Falls City Hall. Thirteen had been killed at the ill-fated lodge meeting; two candidates, Carrie Baker and William Good, were killed before their initiation; and three other members (Christ Miller, the undertaker; Mary Ryan, the hotel laundress; and Elmer Barnes) were killed elsewhere in the city.

As the *Courier-Journal* noted at the time, the black population of Louisville suffered severely. Many lived in the path of the tornado, and

Main Street between Eleventh and Twelfth. *Wilburn Stereographs; 99.36.045; Special Collections, University of Louisville.*

as a sub-headline stated in the paper's March 31 edition, "They Lost But Little in Most Cases, But the Little Was Their All." Zion Methodist Church on Twelfth Street was damaged so badly that all that remained was its rear side and its organ, which somehow escaped unscathed. The reader will recall that the three-story Eclipse Hall where the Colored Odd Fellows met was destroyed beyond repair—just as the lodge members almost had the building paid for. But the fraternity was not about to give in to hopelessness. On March 29, the Grand United Order of Odd Fellows met at Zion Baptist Church. Every lodge in Louisville, including

Corner of Eleventh and Market. *Wilburn Stereographs; 99.36.039; Special Collections, University of Louisville.*

the Household of Ruth, the women's branch of the order, pledged to help the Adam Lodge build a new meetinghouse at Thirteenth and Walnut. A large subscription was raised.

Many black residents lost property and were badly injured, but only a few lost their lives. An entire family named Gaddy was killed at Congress Alley, as was James Smith. Lulu Brown was instantly killed when her Eleventh Street house collapsed; Ada Helm, apparently a resident of Elizabethtown, was killed at Eighth and Main; and Walter Davis died at his Pleasant Street home. A young boy named William Welch vanished in the wake of the tornado. There were some hairbreadth escapes. Elvira Smith was at her Congress Alley home with four children when they heard the deafening sound of hail and nearby houses disintegrating. "Grandma, do you hear that wagon?" asked a little boy.

"That is not a wagon but a cyclone," she replied, realizing that the storm was practically upon them. When the house fell apart, Smith told the children, "We can do nothing but trust in the Lord." She dropped to her knees and prayed as windows shattered and walls fell. Smith and the four children survived; three of them were in bed when the storm came, and a reporter declared that "if they had been in their usual place, they would have been killed."

Despite the loss of much property, the black population of Louisville gave generously to the Relief Fund. The members of the Baptist Ministers' and Deacons' Conference took up collections at their respective churches and turned over the sum to Mayor Jacob.

The tornado happened to strike Louisville just before Easter, resulting in one of the grimmest religious holidays in the city's history. Good Friday, April 4, was marked by great solemnity. The altars at Episcopal and Catholic churches were draped in black in memory of Reverend Barnwell and Sister Mary Pius. Attendance was noticeably high at all churches. Special services were held in memory of the storm victims. Bells were not rung and organs were not played. The Palm Sunday following the tornado became known in Louisville history as "the Sunday of funerals." There were so many dead that horses had to move to and from the city's cemeteries at a trot so all could be buried by sundown. There were not enough funeral carriages in Louisville to supply the demand; some tornado victims were carried to their eternal rest in such undignified vehicles as omnibuses and furniture vans draped in black crepe. Notably sad funerals included the services at a cathedral in which five caskets lay side by side, containing the remains of the laundresses killed at the Wright building; they were buried beside one another in St. Louis Cemetery. The funeral for Reverend Barnwell and his son was held at St. Paul's Episcopal Church. They were placed in the same casket, which was decorated with a bouquet of smilax and, as a reference to the religious significance of the day, palms and Easter lilies. Undertaker Christ Miller's services were held at his own funeral parlor. In those days, funerals often were held in private residences rather than in churches or funeral parlors, and many a passerby in Louisville witnessed coffins being carried out of houses by pallbearers, followed by a squad of weeping mourners clad in black. On some occasions, multiple caskets were borne from a particular residence, indicating that several members of a family had been killed.

Reverend Barnwell. *Louisville Courier-Journal*, April 1, 1890. *Courtesy of the* Courier-Journal.

One unexpected result of the tornado was that school attendance dropped for several days after the disaster, especially in the city's west end. Parents were afraid to send their children away in the event that another cyclone should strike. The day after the storm, the high schools were depopulated by half. On March 31, four days after the tornado, it was estimated that only a fourth of the district's children were actually making it to class. One school had such low attendance that the teachers gave up and dismissed the few students who were present.

Scientists, of course, offered their expert opinions on Louisville's disaster. It is fascinating to see, with hindsight granted by more than a century's worth of scientific advancements, what they had right and what they had wrong. One authority quoted in the April 6 *Courier-Journal*, Dr. Daniel Berry of Carmi, Illinois, adhered to the then-common (and still all too common) belief that tornados cannot do maximum damage to a major city. The idea seems to be that cities create updrafts that ward off twisters. But didn't the surreal damage just inflicted on Louisville disprove Dr. Berry's theory? Not at all! Bad as it was, said Berry, had Louisville been a smaller town it would have been far worse. He wrote that the recent experiences suffered by Louisville and St. Louis proved that tornados "can not get in their full work on a compactly built city of substantial structures" because the cityscape "forces the tornado to climb over it, to play at leap-frog, as it were, over the high-shouldered houses." In other words, despite the creaming Louisville got—during which a tornado had enough force to sweep diagonally through the city, cross the Ohio twice and return to the Kentucky shore—Berry felt that cyclones would do more harm to country towns where tornados have more "breathing space" between buildings. It seems not to have occurred to Berry that storm damage would be *less* in towns with a smaller population and fewer structures for a tornado to throw around.

In addition, Berry provided readers with a suggestion that we now know to be very bad advice: since a tornado creates low pressure that makes houses explode, he said, the smart thing to do when a twister approaches is to fasten open all the windows on the side of your house facing away from the tornado. (Another quoted expert, Lieutenant J.P. Finley, agreed with Berry that opening fragile windows is the needful thing to do when a storm with winds of up to three hundred miles per hour is approaching.) Let's hope nobody got killed following this advice. Dr. Berry did have an interesting idea: since low barometric pressure often indicates that the atmospheric conditions are right for making tornados, he suggested that crowded public buildings such as churches and schools be provided with barometers so that people could head for safer quarters when the pressure dropped enough to indicate imminent danger.

In the same issue, Sergeant Frank Burke of the Signal Corps's Louisville office summarized for *Courier-Journal* readers the state of then-current knowledge about the origins of nature's most violent storm. Though Doppler radar was many decades in the future, the Signal Corps in 1890 was adept at predicting roughly where and when tornados would strike. "The conditions under which tornados develop are now so definitely known that the forecasting of their occurrence in a given section of the country has been repeatedly and successfully accomplished by the Signal Office," assured Burke. (Of course, getting that warning out to people in a given area hours in advance, or at least quickly enough to save lives, was another matter. The fastest way to send a warning was by telephone or telegraph, but if a storm destroyed the poles in the affected area—as was the case in Louisville just before chaos broke loose—there was little the Signal Corps could do.) No one could say in 1890 how fast a tornado's winds traveled when at their mightiest; Burke noted that guesses ranged from one hundred miles per hour to one thousand miles per hour (much too high an estimate).

A third expert, Dr. James Lewis Howe, lectured on May 5, 1890, on the subject of tornados in general—the one at Louisville in particular—before the city's Polytechnic Society. He claimed that Kentucky had been hit by seven distinct tornados on March 27. Dr. Howe rightly noted that in order to have optimal conditions for tornado formation, masses of cold, dry, heavy air must conflict with warm, moist, light air. "When the light air once makes an opening through the heavy air above, it rushes up with great rapidity and with a whirling motion, owing to the motion of the storm area," explained Dr. Howe. Centrifugal force created a vacuum in the center of the rotating column. All three experts—Sergeant Burke, Dr. Berry and Dr. Howe—agreed that the Louisville tornado had not actually touched down but had merely passed over close to the ground, as suggested by the fact that it did worse damage to buildings' upper floors than their lower ones; if it had made contact with the earth, they said, then you would have seen some *real* destruction!

After the initial shock, people began to comprehend the magnitude of the disaster that had befallen them, and survivors had plenty of horror stories to tell. A young man had stopped a patrol wagon at the corner of Tenth and Market Streets and climbed inside to see the dead being taken to the city hospital. He found his mother inside.

Captain James Nuttall of the No. 8 Fire Company spent the night fighting blazes with his men, unaware that his mother had been killed at his Jefferson Street house. A reporter described the scene when a messenger found Captain Nuttall and gave him the news: "[W]ith a breaking heart, he had to leave his brave boys and go to his sacred dead."

Jennie Whitman was in a building beside the ill-fated Falls City Hall. When the tornado demolished the hall, Mrs. Whitman crawled through a third-floor window in a blind panic. Pedestrians watched as she clung to the windowsill, her feet resting on the cornice of a window below. People shouted encouragement to her to hold on, but before help arrived she let go and fell into a pile of bricks, breaking her back. Her husband, police officer Louis Whitman, arrived on the scene just in time to see her fall. The building from which Mrs. Whitman fell suffered only a missing roof. Had she stayed put in her room on the third floor, she would have been unharmed.

Frederick Clarence "Bud" Lusher of the Eagle Brass Works was sitting in his office with the firm's engineer when they heard neighboring

Tenth and Market. *Wilburn Stereographs; 99.36.041; Special Collections, University of Louisville.*

buildings being destroyed. The engineer ran to the rear of the office and was saved; Lusher stepped out into the street and was crushed under a falling roof.

While the storm brought tragedy to some, others thanked Providence for saving them from what seemed to be certain death. In some cases, their close calls were so close as to border on the incredible. George W. Custer's family lived in a tiny home at 1108 West Green Street. When the tornado "crushed in the rear like an egg shell," the frightened occupants headed for the front door. Mr. Custer insisted that they remain inside. Seconds later, the top of the front wall collapsed into the yard. Had the Custers gone out the front door, they would have been crushed as though by a gigantic flyswatter.

A Mr. Hill of Henry County and a clerk named Pat Raidy were having a conversation in front of the Enterprise tobacco warehouse when the winds came. Raidy was carried seventy-five feet and died of his injuries; Hill managed to grab one of the warehouse's doorknobs. Hill was whipped around considerably, but both the knob and his iron grip held. When the wind finally died down, Hill was lowered gently to the ground. Obviously, they knew how to make doorknobs in those days.

The infant of a coal boat pilot named George McBride was asleep on the second floor of its West Chestnut Street house when the tornado came. The baby was flung down to the cellar of the collapsing house—but a sofa cushion broke its fall. It was found frightened but uninjured in a debris-filled corner.

A professor named Brooks was in Pendleton, Henry County, when he received a telegram informing him that his Jefferson Street house had been destroyed and all his family killed. He hurried back to Louisville and found that only the first half of the telegram was correct.

Mr. and Mrs. W.N. Little had been entertaining a party of twelve at their Chestnut Street house. The group had just left the dining room when an uninvited guest tore off the wall and threw it across the yard. Had they remained in the room, it is likely everyone would have been killed.

Thomas Sayers and his family were staying at the Louisville Hotel when one wall of their room began to crack and sway. Sayers grabbed his wife and child and ran into the hotel's corridor just as the wall collapsed entirely, landing on Virgil Wright's cigar store below.

When the tornado hit Jerry Tierney's saloon on the corner of Market and Eleventh, the icebox supported the building's two sagging upper floors. Tierney and his patrons escaped by crouching and crawling out.

Workmen at Falls City Hall found a hat bearing the name Philip G. Kern and assumed that his body was buried in the wreckage. However, a *Courier-Journal* reporter found Kern among the living and eager to tell how he had escaped death. He had been waltzing with Minnie Henry at Miss App's dancing school when the story above collapsed on them. Kern and Miss Henry were thrown to the floor. By a mysterious dispensation of Providence, a sturdy table from the third floor landed atop them, right side up. The dancers and the protecting table crashed through the floor into the building's basement. The table sheltered them from falling debris and left an air pocket that provided them oxygen. Kern managed to pick his way through the bricks to safety; soon afterward, workmen rescued Minnie.

A traveling cutlery salesman from Philadelphia, Charles Hessenbruck, was reportedly killed at Wright's cigar store, but he actually was carried across the street by the wind. He managed to grab a chain attached to

Twelfth and Jefferson. *Wilburn Stereographs; 99 36.046; Special Collections, University of Louisville.*

a fireplug and held onto it "like grim death," to employ his own phrase, when a stray roof landed on him. He crawled out from under it, uninjured, and after aiding a little girl who was "more scared than hurt," he went to his hotel room. Back at the destroyed cigar store, rescuers uncovered a corpse that bore a strong resemblance to Hessenbruck and shared his taste in clothing. When he was apprised of the mix-up, he notified his wife and employers that he was not dead.

Thomas Levi, a resident of Noblesville, Indiana, was visiting Louisville on March 27. He had stepped out of a streetcar when the storm "sent the car and mules rolling over and over as if they had been mere toys." Mr. Levi saved himself from a similar fate by throwing himself to the ground and holding the streetcar rails.

Mr. Morris, an agent for the Daisy Railroad, and his entire family lived in the depot building at Parkland. Although the roof was lifted off and the rest of the structure "scattered in all directions," somehow the Morris family escaped with mere bruises.

A severe tornado leaves behind evidence of its strength, hence the photos we have all seen of autos wrapped around trees and straws driven intact into boards. The twister that hit Louisville picked up a three- by eight-inch scantling timber at Falls City Hall, sent it flying three hundred yards and embedded it like an arrow into the front door of the Arlington Hotel.

A frame house on Sixteenth Street had numerous planks stuck into its side as though driven there by a cannon blast. They were too firmly stuck to be pulled out; they would have to be cut out with a hatchet.

For days, articles belonging to tornado victims were picked up in distant sections of the city and parts beyond. These items included light freight such as bed quilts, pillows, comforters, a couple dozen umbrellas, hats and coats, but also heavier things like mattresses. Twenty-five shawls were found, all torn to shreds. Such articles were taken to Central Station, where they were to be claimed by survivors or relatives of the deceased. Eventually, the pile almost reached the ceiling.

A coat and hat belonging to Falls City Hall victims George Huber and Ben McAtee, respectively, were found hanging from a broken telegraph pole on Main Street.

Scraps of paper and documents from Louisville were found at LaGrange, Oldham County. A Mr. Bepler, who lived twelve miles west of Cincinnati, found a check for $522.70, issued by the Falls City Bank of Louisville. It was assumed that the tornadic winds had carried the check there.

At the Blatz and Krebs Stoneworks at Fourteenth and Walnut, the tornado showed off by lifting an enormous, heavy "traveler" (a machine used for carrying blocks of marble), carrying it over one hundred feet and smashing it to pieces on the ground.

The tornado decorated a warehouse at Tenth and Main by sticking a clock onto its wall. "The back of the clock had hung on a nail, and it was as securely fastened as if it had been placed there by hand," said a contemporary account. It had stopped at 8:20 p.m.

A woman standing in the doorway of the Randall house at Eighteenth and Maple was lifted by the wind and thrown against a telegraph pole sixty feet away. The news article does not state if she survived.

The fourth floor of the Tapp, Leathers, and Co. building vanished completely. No trace of the distinctive-looking structure was found in the nearby debris on the street. It was concluded that the tornado must have demonstrated its playful disposition by dropping it in the Ohio River.

At Parkland, the tornado displayed its sense of humor by breaking off an iron lamppost and depositing it in George Grant's yard with such gentility that the glass was not broken or even cracked.

The telegraph poles on the south side of Jefferson Street were bent at a thirty-five-degree angle; the poles on the north side, on Market Street, still stood upright but were completely missing their wires.

In the end, how many were killed by the tornado and what was the amount of the property damage? The earliest estimates were that 150 had been killed and that the city had suffered $1 million worth of damage. It turned out that the human toll was overestimated and the monetary toll underestimated. Three days after the storm, the number of casualties was downgraded to 92. It was continuously revised downward, and in the end, the official death toll was 76. However, people continued to die of tornado-related injuries long after the March 27 disaster. Saloonkeeper Engelbert Schell, a member of the Knights and Ladies of Honor, was internally injured at Falls City Hall but did not succumb to his wounds until March 31; Sarah Wahl died of her injuries in October; and James Whittingham died in November. A few people were not directly killed by the storm but died of tornado-related ailments. My research indicates that the actual toll was well over 100 (see appendix). In addition to deaths, at least 200 people were injured, some so severely that their names appeared in newspaper columns after the storm followed by notations such as "fatally injured" and "will die."

The tornado partially or completely destroyed five churches, the railroad depot, two public halls, three schools, 256 stores, thirty-two factories, eleven tobacco warehouses and 532 residences. The value of damaged property and lost income was obviously much harder to estimate than the number of lives taken; the estimates have fluctuated wildly over the years. On March 30, 1890, the *Courier-Journal* offered losses of $2 million as a conservative estimate. A week later, on April 5, the newspaper admitted that it was impossible to accurately estimate the cost of the tornado. "There is direct loss and indirect loss. Most estimates do not include the latter," a reporter explained. For example, the water company lost $25,000 due to the damaged standpipe. But the temporary loss of water did financial harm to many Louisville factories, which had to shut down and lay off employees for a week. The indirect loss to the city caused by the suspension of the water supply alone might have cost $100,000. As for direct loss, estimates ranged from $1 million to $5 million. The most commonly offered estimate was $2.5 million. The modern equivalent of this sum would be nearly $60 million.

As time passed, the city recovered on both public and private levels. By April 2, most of the wreckage had been cleared away; one notable exception were the still-untouched ruins of St. John's Episcopal Church, where Reverend Barnwell and his son had died. The women of Louisville started a fund to purchase a house for the widow Barnwell. Within a week of the disaster, the various Episcopal congregations had raised $2,000 for her. She also received $5,000 in insurance.

The vestry of the destroyed St. John's had a choice: rebuild the church or disband and join other parishes. They chose to rebuild. Remarkably, after debris had been cleared out of the ruined church's Sunday school room, parishioners held "solemn and impressive" services in that eerie setting on Easter Sunday, April 6. Services were conducted by Reverend Robert Barnwell of Selma, Alabama, the late pastor's brother. His sermon was based on John 11:23: "Thy brother shall rise again." On the first anniversary of the tornado, Reverend Barnwell's parishioners broke ground for the construction of a new $30,000 church on the site of the old one. The cornerstone was laid on May 26, 1891. It read: "To the Glory of God and in loving memory of Stephen Elliott Barnwell who lost his life in the ruins of the old church." Inside the cornerstone was placed a copperplate box containing, among documents relating to the Episcopalian faith, Reverend Barnwell's Bible and prayer book. The church elders also put in an account of the tornado written by Bishop Thomas Dudley, a description of Barnwell's funeral from the *Churchman* of April 19, 1890, a copy of Bishop Dudley's funeral oration and clippings from the *Courier-Journal* relating to the tornado and the Barnwells' funeral.

Ten days after the disaster, the ruins of the Union Depot had been cleared away. The city vowed that a larger building would be erected in its place, and work began on reconstruction almost as soon as the area was cleared. A year after the tornado, Louisville could boast of having "one of the finest railroad stations in the South," a four-story brick depot with every modern convenience. A reporter wrote, "It may be said to be a monument to the cyclone's work."

Members of the black chapter of Odd Fellows and its sister organization, the Household of Ruth, had expressed determination to rebuild their lodge. After the tornado, they picked through the wreckage at Thirteenth and Walnut and salvaged whatever was salvageable; there wasn't much. The lodge's organ had vanished without a trace. Members of both organizations contributed to a fund for reconstructing the lodge on its old location. Furthermore, showing the spirit of self-reliance that distinguished the entire city after the disaster, they desired to raise all the money by themselves and not ask lodges outside the city for help. By April 6, $1,000 had been raised; a year after the tornado came an announcement that "on the same lot a new hall will soon stand, better than before."

The city's waterworks' pumping station was rebuilt at a cost of $400,000. The improved design no longer used a standpipe but rather two air chambers that allowed water to be pumped directly to the reservoir through the city mains.

Within a year of the tornado, a new Falls City Hall had been built. The lodges of various fraternal organizations, including the Masons and the Knights of Pythias, continued to meet there. It is to be assumed that they abandoned the building at the first sign of threatening weather. Next door to the hall was a handsome new three-story house owned by Louis Simm, whose two children and clerk George Foster had been killed in Miss App's dance studio in the old Falls City Hall and who also had lost his home and business in the tornado. Life went on.

In May 1890, William T. Rolph, chairman of the Board of Trade's Relief Committee and one of the true heroes who emerged in the wake of the tornado, spoke of the disaster before the National Conference of Charities and Corrections in Baltimore. He described the efforts of the city businessmen to organize relief for the storm's victims by first providing basic necessities such as food, coal and first aid; next, by providing temporary shelter; and lastly, by providing money for home repairs. The Relief Committee had employed an ingenious indexed ledger containing the names of applicants in order to ascertain that the needy were attended to promptly and also to prevent humbugs from taking advantage of the disaster and the generosity of others to get a handout. In this way, Louisville was able to tend to its own without beseeching help from the state or federal government or other cities. (The committee aided individuals but did not compensate merchants for their losses, feeling that this was beyond the bounds of the charity's intentions.) In Rolph's words, "Louisville paid in full all losses sustained by the tornado by those who could not themselves do so." The system

Ruins of the Church of the Sacred Heart, where Sister Mary Pius was killed. *Louisville Courier-Journal*, April 6, 1890. *Courtesy of the* Courier-Journal.

Statue of the Virgin Mary that escaped the destruction. *Wilburn Stereographs; 99.36.002; Special Collections, University of Louisville.*

had accomplished its humanitarian goals and was efficient to boot: the cost of distributing the funds was less than 1 percent of the money raised.

On March 27, 1891, the first anniversary of the Great Tornado, two memorial services were held in Louisville: one at St. Paul's Episcopal Church in memory of Reverend Barnwell and the other at Warren Memorial Church. The former service featured a performance of Mozart's "Requiem"; the latter featured a speech from Governor Buckner and other dignitaries. "The purpose is appropriately to commemorate an experience that can be recalled only with grief for those who perished, and with gratitude for those who responded so promptly and generously to the calls for relief," said a *Courier-Journal* editorial. A sum of nearly $30,000 was raised at the Warren Memorial Church's nondenominational ceremony for the Children's Free Hospital—a striking example of a community making good come from evil.

A year after the storm, the ruined district had recovered so completely that it was said that a stranger would be unable to tell where the tornado's path had been. Beautiful new mansions stood where there had been ruins. Even the humble cottages of the less affluent were clearly superior to, and more modern than, the houses that had been destroyed. The workingmen's neighborhoods in southwestern Louisville had been notably full of decrepit and old-fashioned residences before the tornado; now, the same neighborhoods had a "fresh, healthy look." In the words of a reporter, "In this respect the disaster was not a disaster."

Next to the Louisville Hotel, where Virgil Wright's store had been—where five laundresses and five patrons had died—there stood a proud five-story store, described by a reporter as "one of the most beautiful in the city." Improved versions of nearly all the ruined tobacco warehouses were built. A three-story solid brick building was constructed on the corner of Eleventh and Market, where three men were killed and their corpses burned in John Thierman's saloon. The park at Baxter Square, which had seemed a hopeless tangle of uprooted trees and debris, was eventually cleaned. New trees were planted, and it is one of Louisville's most beautiful sites to this day. Sacred Heart Church—Father Disney's pride and joy and the site where Sister Mary Pius died—remained a ruin a year after the storm, but before the year 1891 came to a close, construction had begun on a bigger, better church. The missing fingertip on the otherwise unscathed statue of the Virgin Mary was restored in 1958.

In the death-obsessed nineteenth century, it was common for relatives to send "memorial poetry" to the local newspaper for publication on the anniversary of a loved one's demise. As one might expect, the March 29, 1891 *Courier-Journal* included commemorative elegies written by Nick Sullivan's father, mother and brother; John Emerich's wife and children; Louis and Geneva Simm's mother; Peter Fuller's wife and children; Elmer Barnes's parents; Annie Niles's daughter; John Renouf's wife; Fred Depp's three sisters; Charles Schafer's wife and sons; Thomas Puff's wife and children; and Mary Hassan's husband and children. There was also a prose testimonial written by Will Diemer and Nick Sullivan's fellow employees at the Pullman Car Company. None of it was very good, judged by the exacting standards of immortal literature; but if writing it made the bereaved families feel better and enabled them to cope with their losses, then by that criteria it was great poetry.

Two of the last survivors seriously injured by the tornado both died in 1905: Stephen "Tom" Smith, who had worked at the Union Depot and had had his hip crushed when the roof fell, died in April. He had been lame for the remainder of his life but had returned to work at the depot and was one of the most popular men in Louisville. William Wells, a former Union soldier, died in September. When Falls City Hall collapsed, he had sustained fractures of the legs and ribs, but he died of a mere throat ailment.

The terror inspired by the storm lasted long after 1890. A schoolteacher named Minnie Anderson was hit on the head by debris during the tornado, resulting in a slow decline into madness; she was confined to an asylum in March 1899. Mrs. Charles Gilmore of Jeffersonville, Indiana, was so traumatized by the tornado that she died of fright during a thunderstorm on August 12, 1899. Memorial services for the victims were held almost every year until a generation came along that had no firsthand memories of the tornado. In 1898, the Knights and Ladies of Honor held a "cyclone day." For many years, the *Courier-Journal* ran commemorative articles about the storm around every March 27. Insurance companies could be counted on to run scary ads in the spring, reminding Louisvillians of what they had once faced. The German Insurance Company ran an ad in the *Courier-Journal* on the tornado's anniversary in 1915: "THAT AWFUL CYCLONE, March 27, 1890, devastated many homes, stores, factories and churches, thus wiping out the savings of many years in a few minutes. We Have Windstorms Every Spring!" A Louisville bank used the tornado as a cautionary tale in a *Courier-Journal* advertisement as late as July 1958.

Baxter Square Park. *Wilburn Stereographs; 99.36.007; Special Collections, University of Louisville.*

And, of course, for years after the Great Tornado, citizens understandably became nervous when the skies darkened. A cyclone passed over the city on the night of November 25, 1895, belting the town with winds of seventy miles per hour. It only damaged some roofs and signs, but people kept the Weather Bureau busy answering phone calls asking if it was safe to go to sleep. The *Courier-Journal* theorized in May 1899 that some unknown miscreant had gotten into a habit of starting false tornado rumors, presumably just for the joy of frightening his fellow humans. Louisville was visited by violent storms on May 13, 1902; June 28, 1902; March 23, 1903; and March 25, 1904. The June 1902 storm resulted in a man being crushed to death under a falling

Entrance to Baxter Square Park. Note what the tornado's winds did to the fence's three-inch iron rods. *Wilburn Stereographs; 99.36.008; Special Collections, University of Louisville.*

streetcar barn. On January 22, 1904, a violent cyclone passed over the city but did not touch down. On March 27, 1905, the weather conditions in Louisville were identical to the conditions that had created the Great Tornado of exactly fifteen years before; fortunately, nothing happened. A thunderstorm that knocked over trees, lifted roofs and caused the death of one man occurred on July 9, 1907. It was deemed the most serious storm to strike the city since the Great Tornado; luckily, it passed through a sparsely populated area. Had its path been a half mile farther to the east, it might have resulted in many fatalities. On March 27, 1911—the twenty-first anniversary of the storm—Louisville was hit with high winds that caused many a palm to sweat. A storm featuring winds of up to seventy-two miles per hour hit the city on May 25, 1915; it rendered some families homeless but caused no deaths. In each of these cases, panic ensued among people who remembered the tornado of 1890.

On March 25, 1930—forty years after the tornado—people who had survived the collapse of Falls City Hall held a reunion at Aurora Hall.

(The meeting was arranged by A.J. Reed of Lexington, who had been on the building's fourth floor when the tornado struck.) The few attendees held a memorial service and, if human nature holds true, secretly felt guilty because they had escaped while others had not.

The number of survivors of the Great Louisville Tornado dwindled with each passing year. Among the last were John Ph. Kern, Lillian Stege, Neville Bullitt, Walter Bickel, Will M. Smith and Joseph Hardesty. Seventy-nine-year-old printer Kern was interviewed by the *Courier-Journal* in 1952. He was eighteen in 1890. His aunt had been in Falls City Hall but had received only a couple of broken ribs. "I hope I never see another cyclone," he commented. "They said the janitor at the Falls City Hall [J. Fletcher] stayed upstairs while his son went down to close everything up because a storm was a-comin'. The janitor was killed outright and the son lived another forty years!" One of Kern's prized possessions was a framed steel-engraved illustration of the tornado, made in Chicago in 1890.

The detail that stuck in elderly Lillian Stege's mind was that it had been "very, very hot indeed on the afternoon of the tornado, but the next morning it was bitterly cold."

Neville Bullitt, eighty-five years old when interviewed in 1959, was playing cards with his brother and two uncles in a house on River Road with eighteen-inch-thick double brick walls. The tornado missed them on its initial run but struck the house after it crossed the Ohio and came back to destroy the waterworks. Bullitt remembered that the house began shaking, and nine out of a dozen panes shattered in the front window. The house suffered no worse damage but was surrounded by floodwater; Bullitt had to go to church in a rowboat the following Sunday.

Walter Bickel, eighty-three in 1959, lived at Twenty-second and Cedar in 1890. He was close enough to the tornado's path to watch trees lean in the wind and touch buildings. He recalled seeing ten separate fires in the city that had broken out in the wake of the tornado.

Twenty-four-year-old Will M. Smith of Pond Creek, Pike County, had been visiting Louisville on that March 27. Remembering the storm in 1960 at age ninety-four, Smith related that he had arrived with a group of fellow loggers from Catlettsburg, Boyd County. They had breakfast at a tobacco warehouse—likely, one that was destroyed later in the same day. They went to the theatre that night, but the manager came onstage and said, "Well, folks, under the circumstances, it would be just as well if we didn't have the show." Smith and his

Fifteenth and Chestnut. *Wilburn Stereographs; 99.36.047; Special Collections, University of Louisville.*

companions were greatly disappointed and had no idea what the manager was talking about until they walked back to their rooms at the Louisville Hotel and saw wires down. Part of the hotel had collapsed and crushed Virgil Wright's store, killing several people, including the hotel laundresses. "But our rooms hadn't been damaged," remembered Smith, "and they let us go in and stay there." (In the interview, Smith claimed that he and the other loggers had stayed in the famous Galt House, but his memory on this point must have been faulty, as the Louisville Hotel was the one that was partially demolished by the tornado and was located beside Wright's cigar store.) The next day, Smith walked about the ruined district and witnessed bodies being pulled from the wreckage.

In 1890, Joseph DeHam Hardesty, the youngest of thirteen children, lived at 1012 West Jefferson. In a 1963 interview, he remembered that his family had been making popcorn over coals in their living room grate during the violent rain and hailstorm that preceded the tornado. Hardesty's father made a comment about the cessation of the storm when the back door blew into the house and the front wall fell into the lawn. The Hardesty children were of course petrified, but their father calmed them down by saying, "Hush! God Almighty isn't going to hurt you brats." Little Joseph saw not only fires breaking out all over the stricken district but also firemen's horses getting tangled in the wires of downed telegraph poles. The next day, Hardesty's mother took him to an improvised morgue to see the bodies—not to satisfy the child's morbid curiosity but because it was considered a civic duty to help authorities identify tornado victims. "That was the saddest thing I can remember," said Hardesty. "We would step from one body to another but saw no one we knew. It wasn't possible to make an identification of many. They were so mangled."

The survivors of the Great Louisville Tornado, one of the most notorious natural disasters of the nineteenth century, eventually faded away one by one and died. Not so the city itself. It recovered fully after a display of great civic courage and self-reliance, which still inspires more than a century later. The day after the tornado, a *Courier-Journal* reporter made a prediction:

> *When the season of domestic mourning is spent and merchants have disentangled and set up and enlarged their stocks, new homes and warehouses will rise upon fresh foundations, and be added to the fair fame and beauty of the Falls City, and not one vestige of the wreck will remain to offend the eye or recall the harrowing scene that is now displayed.*

He was right.

APPENDIX

List of Louisville Tornado Fatalities

The names of victims as given by Louisville newspapers are presented in alphabetical order. I include this list with the caveat that it is probably not completely accurate. Coroner Miller, who spent a week examining the bodies of the dead—at one point he went seventy hours without sleep—commented in an interview on some of the mistakes on the earliest death lists and the difficulties he faced in making corrections: "Dr. Miller accounts for these errors by the misspelling of names in addition to the numerous wild reports that were continually flying around. In some instances he received as many as three calls to view the same body, the corpse being given a different name each time."

In their excitement and rush to get the story of the tragedy into print, reporters often garbled or repeated the names of the dead. For example, the earliest casualty lists included a Theo Engelmeier, killed at Twenty-third and Market Streets, as well as a Theo Aegleman, also killed at Twenty-third and Market Streets. Due to the similarity of the names and the fact that they both reportedly lost their lives at the same location, I assumed they were the same man. Further research indicated that they were one and the same, and the victim's real name was Theo Angermeier. To give other examples, were William Demar and William Diemer the same person? (It turned out they were.) Were Mrs. Peterson and Mrs. Patterson the same? (Yes.)

The earliest casualty lists included persons who were not dead, such as T. Henry Mason, Hancock County's representative in the Kentucky legislature, who was thought to have been killed at Virgil Wright's store. So-called "dead" people who ended up surprising their friends and relatives included Fannie Rock, Mattie Hogue, brick maker J.P. McCollum, Charles Hessenbruck, Edwin O. Ellis and several others.

More problematic is the case of the James Smith family of Congress Alley. The earliest list, published on March 28, claims that Smith, his wife and their three children all died. On March 29 came two contradictory news articles stating that the Smiths were all dead, but also that the *four* children were alive but badly bruised. On March 30, the entire family was back on the dead list. On March 31, it was announced that the four children were "improving rapidly." The revised list, published on April 2, lists Mr. Smith as the only fatality. Since this was the last word on the subject, I am sticking with the final version.

I have omitted victims listed as "unknown" on the earliest lists on the assumption that they were eventually identified, since there were no later newspaper reports claiming that bodies remained unidentified. Also, I have included persons who died months or even years after the tornado inflicted injuries upon them and who therefore do not appear at all on official death lists in 1890.

Despite its unavoidable inaccuracies, this list can serve as a starting point for researchers and genealogists. I have included alternate spellings of names, street addresses where known (more than one if records are contradictory) and occasional comments. In several instances, I cleared up cases of questioned identity and name spellings by consulting cemetery records. Even allowing for a few victims counted more than once and a few people turning up alive later, the list debunks the official line that "only" seventy-six people died in the tornado.

DEATHS WITHIN THE CITY

1. Angermeier (Engelmeier; Aegleman), Captain Theodore. Twenty-first and Chestnut Streets. Killed at Falls City Hall.
2. Austin, ____. Infant. Walnut and Thirteenth.
3. Baker, Carrie. 1315 Twentieth. Killed at Falls City Hall.
4. Baldwin, White. Police officer. Killed when entering a burning building.
5. Barmen, Jack. Market, near Twelfth. Killed at Falls City Hall.
6. Barnes, Elmer E. 326 Chapel Street. Killed at Eckerle's saloon.

7–8. Barnwell, Reverend Stephen E., rector of St. John's Episcopal Church, and his son Dudley. 1113 West Jefferson.
9. Bauman (Baumer), Jacob. Shoe salesman. Fifteenth and Portland.
10. Bishop, Sallie. 1703 Portland Avenue. Killed at Falls City Hall.
11. Brown, Lulu. 322 Eleventh Street.
12. Campbell, Maggie. Laundress at Louisville Hotel. Killed at Virgil Wright's store.
13. Castleman, Miss. Seventeenth Street.
14. Clifford, William. Market Street (1324 West Madison). Killed at Falls City Hall.
15. Cornell, S. Parker. 1104 West Green Street. Killed at Bisch's store, 1026 Market Street.
16. Crowe, Bridget. Laundress at Louisville Hotel. Killed at Wright's store.
17. Davis (Davies), Moody. Thirteenth and Walnut.
18. Davis, Walter. 617 Pleasant Street.
19. Decker, Richard.
20. Delph, Fritz. 1742 Maple. Killed at Wright's store.
21. Denker, Diedrich. 1528 Lytle. Killed at Falls City Hall.
22. Depp, Fred. Fireman on the C&O Railroad. From Glasgow, Barren County. Killed at John Emerich's store.
23. Diemer (Deemer; Demar), William. Sixteenth and Chestnut. Burned at Thierman's bar, Sixteenth and Magazine.
24–25. Emerich (Emrich; Emerick), John, bartender, and his four-year-old child, Emma. Eighteenth and Maple.
26. Fitzgerald, James. Eighteenth and Maple.
27. Fleischer, August. Master of the Falls City Market. Killed at Falls City Hall.
28. Fletcher, J. Janitor. Twelfth and Jefferson. Killed at Falls City Hall.
29. Foster, George W. Clerk for Louis Simms. 825 Eighteenth. Killed at Falls City Hall.
30. Fuller, Peter. 712 Sixteenth Street. Killed at Falls City Hall.
31–33. Gaddy, Walter; his wife, Maggie; and son Robert. Congress Alley.
34. Geissel, William. Newsboy. Killed at Union Depot.
35. Gifford, William. Madison Street, between Fourteenth and Fifteenth.
36. Good, William H. Twenty-seventh and Bank. Killed at Falls City Hall.
37. Hamilton, John G. 1014 Griffith. Killed at Falls City Hall.
38. Haran, Bridget. Nineteenth and Portland. Killed at Falls City Hall.
39. Hassan, Mary. 215 Seventeenth Street. Killed at Falls City Hall.

40. Hathaway, C.H. From Chicago; also listed as J.D. Hathaway. Killed at Wright's store.
41. Heeb, William. Age nineteen. Twenty-third and Market. Killed at Falls City Hall.
42. Helm, Ada. Killed at home, Eighth and Main.
43. Hill, ____.
44. Hoey, William. Ninth and Jefferson. Killed at Falls City Hall.
45. Hoffstetter (Hoffstatter; Hosetter; Huffsteiter), Emma. Wife of Charles Hoffstetter. 3614 High Street. Killed at Falls City Hall.
46. Horan, Bridget (Mrs. John Horan). 1841 Portland Avenue. Killed at Falls City Hall.
47. Huber, George. Killed at Falls City Hall.
48. Jenks, Charles. 1327 Madison Street (1900 Jefferson). Suffocated in debris at Planters' Warehouse.
49. Johnson, ____. Employed at Ball's.
50. Kelly, Bridget (Sarah). 1805 (1800) High Street. Killed at Falls City Hall.
51. Kelsall, John. 2270 East Walnut Street. Member of Louisville Legion militia band. Killed at Falls City Hall.
52. Kem, Phil G. Western Union Telegraph Company. Killed at Falls City Hall.
53. King, Henry. Rowan Street (Griffith and Twenty-sixth). Killed at Falls City Hall.
54. Kutzleb, Professor Gustave, Sr. 1629 Jackson. Member of Louisville Legion band. Killed at Falls City Hall.
55. Kutzleb, Gustave, Jr. 1629 Jackson. Member of Louisville Legion band. Killed at Falls City Hall.
56. Lazarus, Moses, Jr. 1140 West Market. Killed at Falls City Hall.
57. Lelloff, Belle (Betty). Seventeenth and Lytle. Killed at Falls City Hall.
58. Leugo (Lengs; Lingo; Lango), Henry. Fifteenth Street and Tyler Avenue. Killed at Falls City Hall.
59. Leuker, Dietrich. Killed at Falls City Hall.
60. Lipp (Lipps), Rudolph. 2229 West Walnut Street. Killed at Falls City Hall.
61. Lusher, Frederick Clarence ("Bud"). 315 Ninth Street. Killed at Falls City Hall.
62. Mason, Thaddeus. 410 West Chestnut Street. From Nashville. Killed at Wright's store.
63. McAtee, Ben. Killed at Falls City Hall.
64. McComb, Mary (Margaret). 612 Clean Street.

65. McCue (McCune), Katie. Laundress at Louisville Hotel. Killed at Wright's store.
66. McCulline, James. Eighteenth and Maple.
67. McGinty, Mary. Laundress at Louisville Hotel. Killed at Wright's store.
68. McKee, Dr. Alexander R. From Mercer County (or Danville or Richmond), Kentucky. Killed at Wright's store.
69. McLaughlin, Mary. Nineteenth and Baird (Seventeenth and Baird). Killed at Falls City Hall.
70. McLaughlin, Mr. Eighteenth and Baird.
71. Miller, Christ. Undertaker. Killed at Falls City Hall.
72. Miller, Peter. Sixteenth Street.
73. Mobley, Mrs.
74. Moore, Henry D. Broadway between Sixth and Seventh. Killed at Falls City Hall.
75. Moran, Edward. 208 (225) Twelfth Street. Killed at Planters' Warehouse.
76. Muth, George. Market Street. Killed at Falls City Hall.
77. Niles, Annie E. 1703 (1631) Portland Avenue. Killed at Falls City Hall.
78. Nuttall, Mrs. Jefferson Street, between Eleventh and Twelfth.
79. Paul, Frank. Bartender at Ike Baer's saloon. 2320 West Walnut. Killed at Wright's store.
80. Peady, John.
81. Peterson, Belle. 516 Nineteenth Street. Killed at Falls City Hall.
82. Petty, F. Killed at Falls City Hall.
83. Pius, Sister Mary. Seventeenth and Broadway. Killed at Sacred Heart School.
84. Puff, Tom. 1622 Columbia. Worker at B.F. Avery plow works foundry. Killed at Falls City Hall.
85. Raidy, John. Sixteenth and Grayson. Killed at the Raidy and Woods Tobacco Works.
86. Raidy, Pat. Clerk for S.E. Edmunds.
87. Randolph, B.F. Seventh Street (Seventeenth and Main). Killed at Falls City Hall.
88. Renouf (Reneaut), John. Brother of Mrs. Joseph Niles. 207 Seventeenth Street. Killed at Falls City Hall.
89. Riehl (Reel), John. 749 Fifteenth Street. Killed at Falls City Hall.
90. Ryan, Mary. Laundress at Louisville Hotel. Killed at Wright's store.
91. Sabrie (Sebree), William. Tailor. Chapel Street. Crushed in his bed by collapsing walls of Union Tobacco Factory.

92. Schaefer, Charles. Jackson Street. Brother-in-law of Professor Kutzler.
93. Schell, Engelbert. 321 Twelfth Street. Died on March 31 of injuries sustained at Falls City Hall.
94. Schildt, J.B. (Ben). Undertaker. 339 East Market Street. Burned at Thierman's bar.
95. Schmitt, George. President of the Falls City Market. Market Street. Killed at Falls City Hall.
96. Seibert, Charles. Chapel Street near Main.
97. Senger, Rudolph. 1119 Esquire Street (Twelfth and Zane). Killed at Falls City Hall.
98–99. Simm, Geneva (Genevieve), age five, and Louis Jr., age seven. Children of Louis Simm. Killed at Falls City Hall.
100. Smith, James. Congress Alley, just behind Falls City Hall.
101. Stande, Minnie. Ninth and Chestnut.
102. Stautte, Annie. 914 West Chestnut. Killed at Falls City Hall.
103. Steftan, U.
104. Stephens, John (James) M. 803 West Jefferson. Killed at Falls City Hall.
105. Stephens (Stephan), William. 1613 Pirtle Street. Killed at Falls City Hall.
106. Steubling, Professor Andrew. 529 (526) East Madison. Killed at Falls City Hall.
107. Sullivan, Nicholas James. Magazine Street near Sullivan. Burned at Thierman's bar.
108. Wahl, Sarah. Wife of Jacob Wahl. 1931 Grayson Street. Injured at Falls City Hall; died on October 16, 1890.
109. Whitman, Jennie. Fell from a window in a building next to Falls City Hall.
110. Whittingham, James. Twenty-fifth and St. Cecilia Streets. Injured at Falls City Hall; died on November 12, 1890.
111. Williams, ____. Congress Alley.

ADDITIONAL DEATHS OUTSIDE CITY LIMITS

1. Crowley, ____. Infant daughter of James Crowley. Occurred on John G. Barrett's farm.
2. Kleher (Kleber), Theesie. Daughter of Casimir Kleher. Killed on Thomson's farm three and a half miles from Louisville, south of Parkland.

POSSIBLE VICTIM

1. Welch, William. 2827 Portland Avenue. Disappeared on the evening of the tornado and was never seen again.

DEATHS CAUSED INDIRECTLY BY THE TORNADO

1. Dugan, Annie. 1017 Sixth Street. Sixteen years old, she died of a pulmonary ailment on March 29, 1890, but her obituary states that her medical troubles were "hastened by the horrors of the tornado."
2. Hamm, Margaret. 1122 West Market. Lived a few doors away from Falls City Hall. Her house was destroyed, but she appears to have been only mildly injured, if at all. However, she received a "nervous shock" from which she never recovered. Her health declined until she died on April 17, 1891.
3. Rooney, Sally. Thirteenth and Broadway. Had consumption but allegedly "died of fright" caused by the storm a few days after the disaster.
4. Sternberg, Bernard. Tailor. 726 West Market Street. Sternberg lived next door to Falls City Hall. He was uninjured by the tornado but received a nervous shock so great that he was an invalid for the remaining eighteen years of his life. He died on May 25, 1908.
5. Whalen, Ellen. Sixteenth and Owen. Shortly after the tornado, she died of heart disease exacerbated by fear.

Bibliography

PART I

Tornados in General

Erck, Amy. "Answers Archive: Tornado History, Climatology: When and where was the first tornado recorded in the United States?" *USA Today*, May 30, 1997. http://www.usatoday.com/Weather/resources/askjack.watorhty.htm.

Grazulis, Thomas. *Significant Tornadoes 1880–1989*. Vol. 1. St. Johnsbury, VT: Environmental Films, 1991.

———. "The Tornado Project Online Website." http://www.tornadoproject.com.

Louisville Courier-Journal. "Cyclones," June 14, 1879, 4.

———. "Gunning for Cyclones," June 25, 1899, III, 5.

———. "It Isn't Wind," September 2, 1877, 2.

———. "To Blow Them Up," June 7, 1896, II, 1.

———. "Tornado-Proof," April 12, 1890, 2.

———. "Walls Against Tornados," June 14, 1896, III, 2.

Kentucky Tornados in General

CAVE CITY, KY

Collins, Richard, and Lewis Collins. *History of Kentucky*. Vol. 1. Frankfort: Kentucky Historical Society, 1966. Reprint of 1874 edition.

PITTSBURG, KY

Echo [London, KY]. "The Merciless Elements," March 28, 1884, 3.

———. "Pittsburgh," April 18, 1884, 3.

———. "Pittsburgh," May 9, 1884, 3.

Louisville Courier-Journal. "In Laurel County," March 29, 1890, 6.

———. "A Kentucky Cyclone," March 26, 1884, 1.

———. "The Pitiless Elements," March 26, 1884, 4.

WKYT.com. "Tornado Touchdown Confirmed in Laurel County," November 15, 2007. http://www.wkyt.com/home/headlines/11308506.html.

COLEMANSVILLE, KY

Louisville Courier-Journal. "The Pitiless Elements," March 26, 1884, 4.

———. "The Storm Swept," March 27, 1884, 4.

CLINTON AND WICKLIFFE, KY

Grazulis, Thomas. *Significant Tornadoes 1880–1989.* Vol. 1. St. Johnsbury, VT: Environmental Films, 1991.

Louisville Courier-Journal. "Clinton's Calamity," January 19, 1890, 15.

———. "Wind and Death," January 14, 1890, 1.

Louisville Tornados, Pre-1890, and Events Just Before the 1890 Storm

Collins, Richard, and Lewis Collins. *History of Kentucky.* Vol. 1. Frankfort: Kentucky Historical Society, 1966. Reprint of 1874 edition.

Landau, Herman. "A March Wind That Was All Lion." *Louisville Courier-Journal*, March 28, 1937, Magazine, 2.

Louisville Courier-Journal. "Almost a Horror," March 11, 1873, 4.

———. "'Cyclone' Anniversary Falls Tomorrow Night," March 26, 1911, II, 3.

———. "A Cyclone Scare," May 17, 1886, 8.

———. "The Last Accident," March 12, 1873, 4.
———. "Letter Recalls Horrors of Louisville Cyclone: John Doyle, Former Resident…," March 30, 1938, I, 2.
———. "A Night of Horror," March 28, 1891, 12.
———. "Not the First Tornado," April 3, 1890, 6.
———. "A Sou'wester," November 29, 1879, 4.
———. "Terrible Tornado," May 22, 1860, 1.
———. "The Tornado," May 24, 1860, 1.
———. "Tornado," March 28, 1890, 1.
———. "The Tornado Monday!" May 23, 1860, 1.
Trout, Allan. "Greetings." *Louisville Courier-Journal*, October 4, 1962, II, 23.

PART II

Clark, Francis P. Letter to the editor. *Louisville Courier-Journal*, March 27, 1957, I, 8.
Harriman, J.S. "The Big Blow." *Louisville Courier-Journal*, March 23, 1958, Magazine, 21–24.
Landau, Herman. "The Great Tornado." *Louisville Courier-Journal*, March 27, 1939, Magazine, 14–18.
———. "A March Wind That Was All Lion." *Louisville Courier-Journal*, March 28, 1937, Magazine, 2.
Louisville Courier-Journal. "At Wright's Store," March 29, 1890, 8.
———. "Barnwell Tragedy," April 6, 1890, 22.
———. "Baxter Square Ruined," April 6, 1890, 13.
———. "Broadway," March 30, 1890, 19.
———. "Burned to Death," March 28, 1890, 4.
———. "By the Flames," March 28, 1890, 4.
———. "Chestnut Street," March 29, 1890, 4.
———. "Colored People," March 31, 1890, 7.
———. "The Cross Streets," March 29, 1890, 9.
———. "The Fated Structure," April 6, 1890, 21.
———. "Fire and Death," April 6, 1890, 6.
———. "Grayson Street," April 6, 1890, 22.
———. "The Great Tornado: Sgt. Frank Burke Gives a Scientific Account," April 6, 1890, 17.
———. "Green Street," April 6, 1890, 19.

———. "Hessenbruck Alive and Well," April 1, 1890, 2.
———. "Horror! The Frightful Calamity at Falls City Hall," March 28, 1890, 1.
———. "Jefferson Street," April 6, 1890, 20.
———. "Jeffersonville," March 28, 1890, 3.
———. "Madison Street," April 6, 1890, 22.
———. "Magazine Street," March 29, 1890, 4.
———. "Main Street," April 6, 1890, 7.
———. "Main Street's Tragedy," March 28, 1890, 2.
———. "Market Street," April 6, 1890, 4.
———. "A More Cheerful Outlook." Editorial, April 2, 1890, 4.
———. "New Albany Escaped," March 28, 1890, 3.
———. "A Night of Horror," March 28, 1891, 12.
———. "On Chestnut Street," March 28, 1890, 3.
———. "On Main Street," March 28, 1890, 2.
———. "On Market Street," March 28, 1890, 3.
———. "On the River," March 29, 1890, 8.
———. "Out of the City," March 29, 1890, 3.
———. "Panic at the Council," March 28, 1890, 3.
———. "Rev. Barnwell's Death," March 28, 1890, 2.
———. "The River," March 28, 1890, 3.
———. "A Scientific Account," March 28, 1890, 3.
———. "A Shocking Incident," March 28, 1890, 3.
———. "Sunday Note-Book: A Survivor's Graphic Description of the Falls City Hall Disaster," April 6, 1890, 13.
———. "The Tobacco District," March 28, 1890, 4.
———. "Told in Brief: The Story of the Great Calamity…," April 6, 1890, 4.
———. "Tornado," March 28, 1890, 1.
———. "A Tornado Lecture," May 6, 1890, 8.
———. "The Tornado's Freaks," March 30, 1890, 4.
———. "The Union Depot," March 28, 1890, 2.
———. "The Union Depot," March 29, 1890, 4.
———. "Walnut Street," March 29, 1890, 4.
———. "Where It Struck: Scott Grove…," April 6, 1890, 22.
Trout, Allan. "Greetings." *Louisville Courier-Journal*, October 4, 1962, II, 23.

PART III

Clowes, Molly. "Louisville Triumphs Over Disaster, '84 and '90 Prove." *Louisville Courier-Journal*, February 11, 1937, I, 2.

Grazulis, Thomas. *Significant Tornadoes 1880–1989*. Vol. 1. St. Johnsbury, VT: Environmental Films, 1991.

Griffin, Gerald. "Storm Skipped 'Uncle' Will." *Louisville Courier-Journal*, April 25, 1960, II, 1.

Harriman, J.S. "The Big Blow." *Louisville Courier-Journal*, March 23, 1958, Magazine, 21–24.

Landau, Herman. "A March Wind That Was All Lion." *Louisville Courier-Journal*, March 28, 1937, Magazine, 2.

Louisville Courier-Journal. "About Insurance," March 29, 1890, 3.

———. Advertisements for various Louisville companies, March 29, 1890, 7; March 31, 1890, 7; September 20, 1891, 17; March 27, 1915, 7; May 26, 1915, 2; May 26, 1915, 7; July 31, 1958, I, 7.

———. "Among the Ruins: Impressive Services…in St. John's Sunday School Room," April 7, 1890, 6.

———. "Anniversary of the Tornado." Editorial, March 27, 1891, 4.

———. "Appalling!" March 29, 1890, 1.

———. "As Others See Us," April 6, 1890, 6.

———. "At St. Paul's," March 28, 1891, 3.

———. "The Baer Building [Virgil Wright's store]," April 6, 1890, 22.

———. "Beautiful Parkland," March 29, 1890, 4.

———. "The Builders' Exchange," April 1, 1890, 7.

———. "Business." Editorial, March 29, 1890, 6.

———. "The Business Situation." Editorial, March 30, 1890, 16.

———. "Calls for Help: Over 800 Applicants for Relief…," April 5, 1890, 8.

———. "Cheerful: Main Street Rapidly Resuming Its Old-Time Activity," April 2, 1890, 6.

———. "Chestnut Street," April 6, 1890, 7.

———. "The City's Boast," April 3, 1890, 4.

———. "Colored Odd Fellows," March 30, 1890, 8.

———. "Colored People," March 31, 1890, 7.

———. "The Coroner's Work," March 30, 1890, 8.

———. "Counting Up," March 30, 1890, 7.

———. "The Cross Streets," March 29, 1890, 9.

———. "The Cut-Off," March 28, 1890, 4.

———. "'Cyclone' Anniversary Falls Tomorrow Night," March 26, 1911, II, 3.
———. "Cyclone Passed Over Louisville Last Night," November 26, 1895, 1.
———. "Cyclone Survivors to Meet Tonight," March 25, 1930, I, 9.
———. "Cyclone Swept City 20 Years Ago Today," March 27, 1910, IV, 7.
———. "Cyclone Victim Insane," March 9, 1899, 7.
———. "Cyclones and Tornadoes." Editorial, March 29, 1890, 6.
———. "Death's Track: The Swath the Tornado Mowed Through Western Kentucky," April 1, 1890, 1.
———. "Death Trap," March 29, 1890, 8.
———. "Destruction," March 28, 1890, 4.
———. "Died of Fright," August 15, 1899, 5.
———. "Drift from the Storm," April 1, 1890, 2.
———. "Energetic Merchants." Editorial, March 31, 1890, 4.
———. "Escape of Miss App," April 6, 1890, 21.
———. "Fair for a Few Hours: Another Tornado Rumor…," May 8, 1899, 2.
———. "Falls City Cyclone Survivors of 1890," March 7, 1930, I, 6.
———. "Falls City Hall," April 6, 1890, 21.
———. "Falls City Hall: Sketch of the Upper Stories," April 2, 1890, 6.
———. "The Fated Structure," April 6, 1890, 21.
———. "Fifteenth Anniversary of the Fatal Cyclone," March 27, 1905, 10.
———. "Fire and Death," April 6, 1890, 6.
———. "The First News: How the Facts of the Catastrophe Were Sent to the World…," April 1, 1890, 8.
———. "For Mrs. Barnwell," April 2, 1890, 6.
———. "For Robbing a Dead Man," April 3, 1890, 7.
———. "For the Sufferers: Net Proceeds of May Day Celebration…," April 1, 1890, 7.
———. "For Sweet Charity: The House Appropriates $30,000…," April 2, 1890, 8.
———. "From Every Side: Board of Trade Relief Committee Receiving Liberal Contributions," April 1, 1890, 6.
———. "Funerals," March 31, 1890, 1.
———. "Giving Aid," March 31, 1890, 2.
———. "A Good Work Well Done," April 1, 1890, 4.
———. "Gray from Fright," March 31, 1890, 2.
———. "The Great Tornado," March 27, 1891, 2.

———. "The Great Tornado: Sgt. Frank Burke Gives a Scientific Account," April 6, 1890, 17.
———. "Half a Million Enough," April 1, 1890, 7.
———. "Hard at Work: Wrecked Homes in the Devastated District Rapidly Becoming Habitable," April 7, 1890, 6.
———. "Help," March 30, 1890, 7.
———. "Helping Hands…," April 2, 1890, 6.
———. "Helping Helpless: Work of the General Relief Committee…," April 3, 1890, 6.
———. "Help Still Coming," March 31, 1890, 7.
———. "A Heroic Farmer," April 4, 1890, 6.
———. "High Winds Cause Many to Remember Cyclone," March 28, 1911, 4.
———. "In Darkness Storm Left the City Last Night," May 14, 1902, 9.
———. "In Memoriam." Memorial poetry, March 29, 1891, 5.
———. "In Memoriam: Resolutions in Regard to the Death of Mr. Barnwell," April 3, 1890, 7.
———. "In Parkland," March 30, 1890, 7.
———. "Insurance Losses," March 30, 1890, 4.
———. "Jefferson Street," March 29, 1890, 3.
———. "Knights of Honor: General Relief Committee…," April 2, 1890, 6.
———. "The Legion on Guard," March 28, 1890, 3.
———. "Lessons of the Storm." Editorial, July 11, 1907, 4.
———. "Letter Recalls Horrors of Louisville Cyclone: John Doyle, Former Resident…," March 30, 1938, I, 2.
———. "The Loss by the Tornado." Editorial, March 29, 1890, 6.
———. "Louisville Just Escaped a Cyclone," January 23, 1904, 2.
———. "Louisville Swept by Big Tornado 49 Years Ago," March 27, 1939, I, 2.
———. "Louisville's Pluck," April 4, 1890, 4.
———. "Louisville's Tornado: Mr. W.T. Rolph Tells of It…," May 17, 1890, 3.
———. "Louisville's Vitality." Editorial, April 4, 1890, 4.
———. "Main Street," April 6, 1890, 7.
———. "Main Street's Loss," March 29, 1890, 3.
———. "Man's Kindness to Man," April 1, 1890, 4.
———. "Market Street," April 6, 1890, 4.
———. "Market Street," March 29, 1890, 3.

———. "Martial Law," March 29, 1890, 4.
———. "Memorial Service," March 18, 1898, 8.
———. "Miscellaneous," March 28, 1890, 4.
———. "Miscellaneous," March 29, 1890, 10.
———. "Miscellany," March 30, 1890, 7.
———. "Mr. Mansfield's Arrival," March 31, 1890, 2.
———. "Narrow Escape," March 29, 1890, 4.
———. "News and Comment," March 30, 1890, 2.
———. "News and Comment: The Summary of Casualties Resulting… Outside of Louisville…," April 6, 1890, 8.
———. "A Night of Horror." Editorial, March 28, 1890, 6.
———. "No Advance in Wages," March 30, 1890, 6.
———. "No Outside Aid Needed." Editorial, March 31, 1890, 4.
———. "No Telegraph Wires," March 28, 1890, 3.
———. "Nothing Could Kill Him," April 4, 1890, 6.
———. "Offers of Relief." Editorial, March 30, 1890, 16.
———. "Official Tenders of Help," March 29, 1890, 8.
———. "On the Breaks: Tobacco Warehouses Not as Badly Damaged…," April 1, 1890, 7.
———. "One of Tornado's Victims Buried Yesterday," September 20, 1905, 2.
———. "Our Mercantile Activity," April 1, 1890, 4.
———. "Parkland Points," April 6, 1890, 6.
———. "Plenty of Water," April 5, 1890, 8.
———. "Preachers at Work," April 1, 1890, 8.
———. "The Precious Fluid," April 4, 1890, 6.
———. "The Property Destroyed." Editorial, March 30, 1890, 16.
———. "The Property Loss," April 6, 1890, 22.
———. "Proposals to Help," March 29, 1890, 8.
———. "Prospective Water Famine," March 29, 1890, 4.
———. "Ready to Relieve: Knights of Honor Organize…," April 1, 1890, 7.
———. "Reanimation: Business Looking Up from Among the Ruins," April 1, 1890, 6.
———. "Recovering," March 30, 1890, 6.
———. "The Red Cross," March 31, 1890, 2.
———. "Relief," March 29, 1890, 1.
———. "The Relief Committee," April 3, 1890, 4.
———. "Relief Measures." Editorial, March 29, 1890, 6.

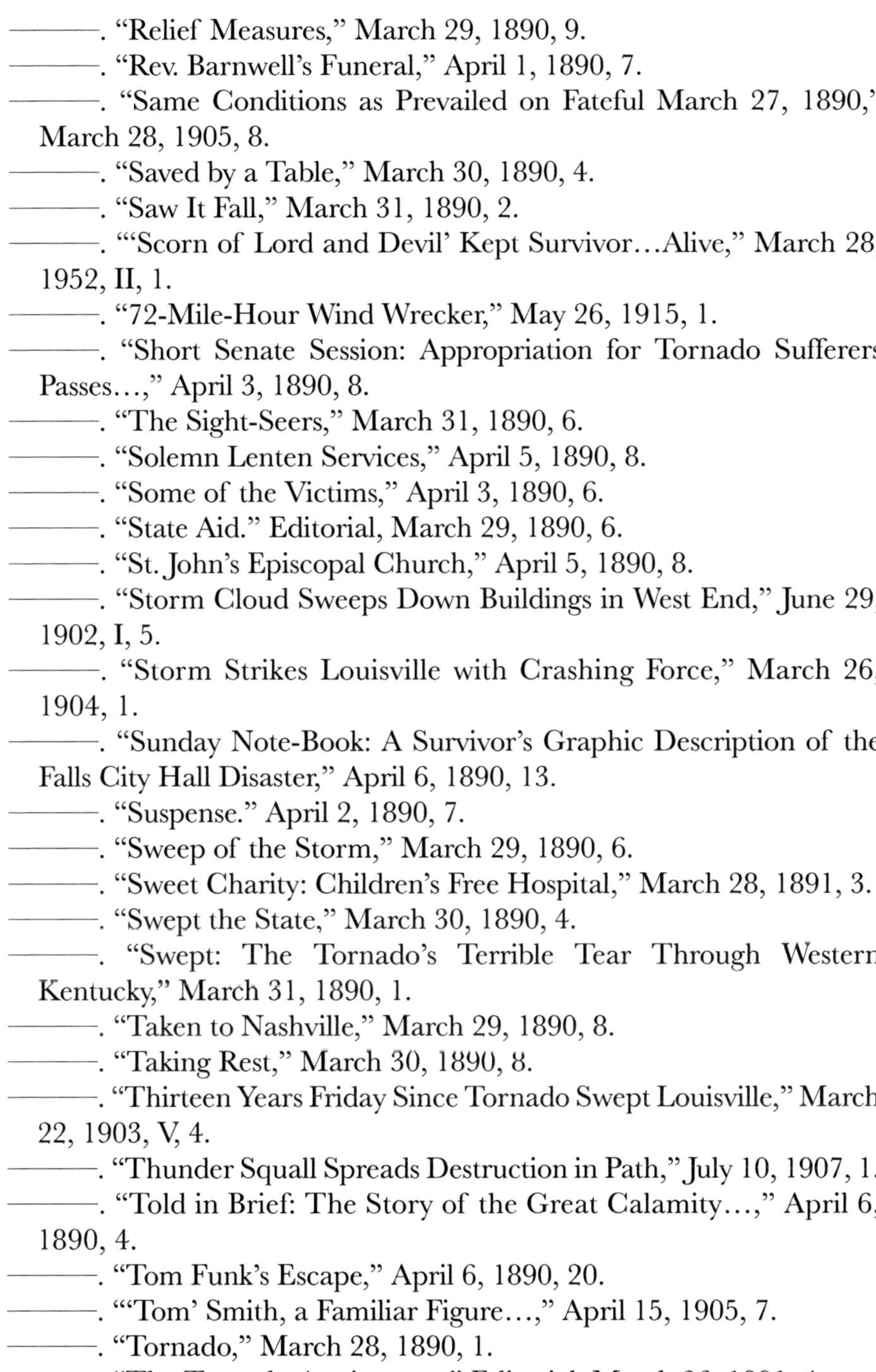

———. "Relief Measures," March 29, 1890, 9.
———. "Rev. Barnwell's Funeral," April 1, 1890, 7.
———. "Same Conditions as Prevailed on Fateful March 27, 1890," March 28, 1905, 8.
———. "Saved by a Table," March 30, 1890, 4.
———. "Saw It Fall," March 31, 1890, 2.
———. "'Scorn of Lord and Devil' Kept Survivor…Alive," March 28, 1952, II, 1.
———. "72-Mile-Hour Wind Wrecker," May 26, 1915, 1.
———. "Short Senate Session: Appropriation for Tornado Sufferers Passes…," April 3, 1890, 8.
———. "The Sight-Seers," March 31, 1890, 6.
———. "Solemn Lenten Services," April 5, 1890, 8.
———. "Some of the Victims," April 3, 1890, 6.
———. "State Aid." Editorial, March 29, 1890, 6.
———. "St. John's Episcopal Church," April 5, 1890, 8.
———. "Storm Cloud Sweeps Down Buildings in West End," June 29, 1902, I, 5.
———. "Storm Strikes Louisville with Crashing Force," March 26, 1904, 1.
———. "Sunday Note-Book: A Survivor's Graphic Description of the Falls City Hall Disaster," April 6, 1890, 13.
———. "Suspense." April 2, 1890, 7.
———. "Sweep of the Storm," March 29, 1890, 6.
———. "Sweet Charity: Children's Free Hospital," March 28, 1891, 3.
———. "Swept the State," March 30, 1890, 4.
———. "Swept: The Tornado's Terrible Tear Through Western Kentucky," March 31, 1890, 1.
———. "Taken to Nashville," March 29, 1890, 8.
———. "Taking Rest," March 30, 1890, 8.
———. "Thirteen Years Friday Since Tornado Swept Louisville," March 22, 1903, V, 4.
———. "Thunder Squall Spreads Destruction in Path," July 10, 1907, 1.
———. "Told in Brief: The Story of the Great Calamity…," April 6, 1890, 4.
———. "Tom Funk's Escape," April 6, 1890, 20.
———. "'Tom' Smith, a Familiar Figure…," April 15, 1905, 7.
———. "Tornado," March 28, 1890, 1.
———. "The Tornado Anniversary." Editorial, March 26, 1891, 4.

———. "The Tornado District," March 29, 1891, 16.
———. "Tornado Forms…What an Authority on the Subject Has to Say…," April 6, 1890, 18.
———. "Tornado Losses to Be Paid," April 1, 1890, 7.
———. "Tornado Memorial Services," March 15, 1891, 9.
———. "Tornado Memorial Services," March 22, 1891, 17.
———. "Tornado Memorial Services," March 26, 1891, 2.
———. "Tornado Relief," April 26, 1891, 9.
———. "The Tornado's Work: Additional Accounts of Disaster [in KY]," April 3, 1890, 2.
———. "The Union Depot," April 1, 1890, 7.
———. "The Union Depot," April 6, 1890, 19.
———. "Was Not Unmixed Evil: Mr. W.T. Rolph Points Out…," July 13, 1890, 16.
———. "The Water Supply," April 1, 1890, 6.
———. "The Water-Works," April 6, 1890, 21.
———. "Water-Works Ruined," March 28, 1890, 3.
———. "The Western Union," March 31, 1890, 7.
———. "What Mr. Clarke Thinks," March 29, 1890, 2.
———. "Where the Tornado Swept: Laying of the Cornerstone of the New St. John's…," May 27, 1891, 8.
———. "Will Make No Advance: Bricklayers Hold a Meeting…," April 1, 1890, 8.
———. "Wind Blows," March 24, 1903, 2.
———. "The Wires Working," March 29, 1890, 4.
———. "With Jewels and Unknown," March 29, 1890, 3.
———. "With Offers of Help," March 29, 1890, 8.
———. "With the Railroads," March 29, 1890, 4.
———. "The Work of Relief," April 1, 1890, 4.
———. "The Work Stopped [at Falls City Hall]," April 1, 1890, 7.
Meehan, John. "Disastrous Louisville Tornado…Is Recalled." *Louisville Courier-Journal*, March 22, 1959, I, 10.
Porter, Marion. "Tornado Killing 76 Here Is Recalled." *Louisville Courier-Journal*, March 26, 1963, II, 1.

APPENDIX

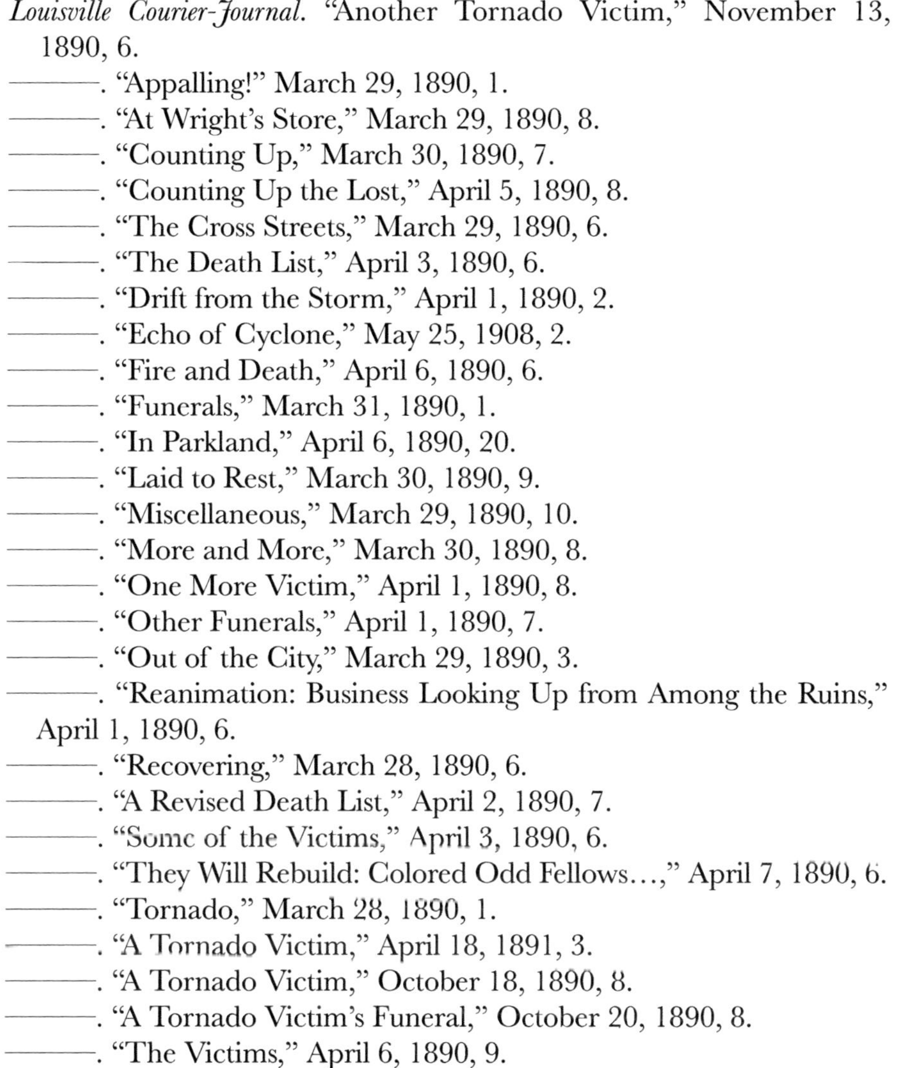

Louisville Courier-Journal. "Another Tornado Victim," November 13, 1890, 6.
———. "Appalling!" March 29, 1890, 1.
———. "At Wright's Store," March 29, 1890, 8.
———. "Counting Up," March 30, 1890, 7.
———. "Counting Up the Lost," April 5, 1890, 8.
———. "The Cross Streets," March 29, 1890, 6.
———. "The Death List," April 3, 1890, 6.
———. "Drift from the Storm," April 1, 1890, 2.
———. "Echo of Cyclone," May 25, 1908, 2.
———. "Fire and Death," April 6, 1890, 6.
———. "Funerals," March 31, 1890, 1.
———. "In Parkland," April 6, 1890, 20.
———. "Laid to Rest," March 30, 1890, 9.
———. "Miscellaneous," March 29, 1890, 10.
———. "More and More," March 30, 1890, 8.
———. "One More Victim," April 1, 1890, 8.
———. "Other Funerals," April 1, 1890, 7.
———. "Out of the City," March 29, 1890, 3.
———. "Reanimation: Business Looking Up from Among the Ruins," April 1, 1890, 6.
———. "Recovering," March 28, 1890, 6.
———. "A Revised Death List," April 2, 1890, 7.
———. "Some of the Victims," April 3, 1890, 6.
———. "They Will Rebuild: Colored Odd Fellows…," April 7, 1890, 6.
———. "Tornado," March 28, 1890, 1.
———. "A Tornado Victim," April 18, 1891, 3.
———. "A Tornado Victim," October 18, 1890, 8.
———. "A Tornado Victim's Funeral," October 20, 1890, 8.
———. "The Victims," April 6, 1890, 9.

About the Author

Other books by Keven McQueen

BIOGRAPHY/HISTORY

Cassius M. Clay, Freedom's Champion (Turner Publishing, 2001)
More Offbeat Kentuckians (McClanahan Publishing, 2004)
Offbeat Kentuckians: Legends to Lunatics (McClanahan Publishing, 2001)

HISTORICAL TRUE CRIME

Cruelly Murdered: The Murder of Mary Magdalene Pitts and Other Kentucky True Crime Stories (Jesse Stuart Foundation, 2008)
Murder in Old Kentucky: True Crime Stories from the Bluegrass (McClanahan Publishing, 2005)
Strange Tales of Crime and Murder in Southern Indiana (The History Press, 2009)

FOLKLORE/HISTORY

Forgotten Tales of Indiana (The History Press, 2009)
Forgotten Tales of Kentucky (The History Press, 2008)
The Kentucky Book of the Dead (The History Press, 2008)

For information, misinformation and disinformation, check out KevenMcqueen.com.